ACTIVATE

Spiritual Exercises to Engage with God
and Become the Church of Acts

Wendy Bowen

DEDICATION

This book is dedicated to the Body of Christ, His Church.
We're in this together.

CONTENTS

INTRODUCTION
Before You Activate

Welcome to ACTIVATE! This is a book of spiritual exercises that guide disciples of Christ to engage with God so that the Church today becomes more like the Church that we read about in the Book of Acts. Each of the Activities in this book help participants to start doing the things that Jesus and His first disciples did.

ACTIVATE is not a book of teaching but a book of doing. It was written to pair well with *ACTS: Activating the Church with the True Gospel and Spiritual Power.* ACTS is for the teaching or hearing of the Word of God and ACTIVATE is for the doing of the Word of God. Each numerical Activity of ACTIVATE corresponds to the Chapter of the same number in ACTS. This said, it is not necessary to read them together and each book can be read or used independent of the other.

Some of the Activities in this book include a brief introduction which is intended to give some background or insight into the Activity or its Scriptural foundation. However, in order to keep ACTIVATE a book of doing, teaching has been kept to a minimum. This said, there are many other books which teach, theologize, and discuss the various schools of thought, methods, and approaches to doing several of the Activities in this book. I encourage you to read them as the Lord leads and as you grow into doing the things that Jesus did in the way that He did them.

ACTIVATE contains some exercises which are intended for beginners or use methods that I refer to as "training wheels." Like training wheels on a bicycle, the intent is to make entry into spiritual activity more accessible for everyone, particularly those who have never engaged with God in these ways before. "Training wheels" are an effective way of reducing potential embarrassment for beginners and this helps people to take the risk of stepping out in faith. But, just like training wheels on a bicycle, once someone enters into the flow of things the training wheels can be removed and, with continual practice, the person is on their way to full proficiency.

The purpose of doing these Activities is to encounter God, experience the power of the Holy Spirit, and embark on a journey towards spiritual maturity or Christlikeness. Jesus modeled the normal Christian life for us by maintaining an abiding relationship of love with God as His Father, living by the guidance and governance of His divine nature, and doing works by the power of the Holy Spirit. The Activities in this book will help Christ followers today to grow into these various aspects of being like Him. If you desire to focus on any of the aspects of Christ's likeness in particular, then here is a listing of the Activities in this book pertaining to each facet of spiritual maturity.

ABIDE IN CHRIST	DIVINE NATURE	WORKS WITH POWER
1: Living the Gospel	5: Death to Life	6: Pentecost
2: Living Word	9: Love One Another	7: Cast Out Demons
3: Communion	11: Love Your Enemies	8: Prophesy
4: Remember His Love	13: Tending Soils	10: Heal the Sick
12: In God's Presence	15: The Aim	14: Teach, Preach, Testify
	16: 40 Day Reset	

ACTIVATE Activities Include

⬧ A brief statement of the Activity's purpose.

⬧ "This Activity will help you to:" A list of how the Activity will help you to grow into Christlikeness.

⬧ Introduction: A brief introduction to the Activity or its Biblical foundation.

⬧ Steps: Instructions for doing the Activity. Instructions flow all the way through from start to finish. Additional materials needed to do the Activity are given at the end of the instructions. (see Actsheets)

⬧ "Onward to maturity:" A description of how to grow in proficiency or when to return to the Activity as you grow in Christ.

⬧ "The aim of this Activity…:" A description of spiritual maturity pertaining to the Activity at hand, which was demonstrated by Jesus.

⬧ Actsheets: Actsheets are worksheets without the work and contain additional materials needed to do any given Activity. See www.activatedchurch.com/actsheets for easily printed pdf versions of all Actsheets.

⬧ Additional Activation: Additional Activities that are relevant to the subject at hand. These can be done in addition to, or in place of, the primary Activity. There are a total of 40 Activities in this book.

Authority in Christ

Some of the Activities of this book teach believers how to step into their Christ-given authority and engage with the power of God through faith in Christ's finished work.[1] Jesus sent His first disciples out with divine power and authority to proclaim the Kingdom of God with signs and wonders following, (see Matthew 10:1, 5-15, 28:18-20; Mark 16:15-20;Luke 9:1-6, 10:1-20) and this is no different for His disciples today.

This said, Jesus warned not to rejoice in God-given authority but to rejoice in right standing with God. Additionally, Jesus taught and demonstrated love, servanthood, and giving freely all of the benefits of salvation, deliverance, healing, and sustenance. These things are the primary aim of several other Activities in this book. We can only give what we have received and we can only love because He first loved us.

May all who encounter God through the Activities of this book follow in the footsteps of Jesus and be obedient to His commands and warnings.

---

[1] For an in-depth study on Kingdom power and authority, see *ACTS: Chapter 7: Kingdom*

Cast Your Cares

The introductory Activity of this book is called *Cast Your Cares*. After taking sufficient time to learn how to *Cast Your Cares* the first time that you do the Activity, I recommend taking a minute or two to do this Activity at the beginning of each of your meeting times. Personally, I *cast my cares* on a daily basis and lead others in doing so before times of teaching, study, or prayer. I have found that when we cast all of our cares on Jesus, we are free to hear more clearly what God cares about and the things that He desires to reveal to us as we engage with Him.

My Prayer for You

My prayer is that this book helps you and your group or church to encounter the love of God, the truth of Christ, and the power of the Holy Spirit in ways that you never have before. In Jesus' name, I declare a supernatural release of the Holy Spirit into your life, your group, and your church so that the Church today becomes just like the Church of Acts.

Blessed are those who hear the Word and do it.[2]

---

[2] Luke 11:28

♦Notes for Leaders

If God has appointed you as the leader over a small group or church, then you have been entrusted with a great responsibility. This said, you needn't feel over-burdened because God is with you and He desires for you and your group to experience His love and Kingdom power through faith in Jesus Christ. Here are a few quick notes that may be helpful to you as you lead your group in these Activities.

Prepare and Stay Alert: Before your group meets to do the Activities, prepare yourself as the leader by reading through the Activity from start to finish and envisioning the group doing each step so that you know what to expect and can lead the group effectively. As you lead your group in the Activities, stay alert to the promptings of the Holy Spirit. God may have something wonderful for you that is not written in the steps of the Activity. This book is to get you started, so don't feel restricted in any way if the Lord leads you to do something a little different.

Grace for Mistakes: Encourage everyone in your group to engage with God to the fullest extent that they are willing and able. Keep God in control but encourage an atmosphere of freedom in the Holy Spirit and allow people to spread their spiritual wings a bit. Everybody makes mistakes when they are growing so give plenty of mercy and grace when mistakes are made. This applies to you as the leader, too.

The Unexpected: Trust that God will show you what to do if you encounter anything unexpected or something that I did not specifically articulate in the instructions of the Activity. Resist fear and seek wisdom from God. When in doubt, stop and pray. Yes, you heard me. If you begin to feel overwhelmed, uncomfortable, or someone in the group is causing unnecessary problems, then you have been given a great opportunity to demonstrate your own humility and dependence upon God. Simply say something like, "Let's take a break for a minute and pray to the Father" or, "Let's stop and listen to the Lord for a moment and see if He has anything to say to us right now." We're all in this together and we're all in need of God's guidance. It's ok to not know everything.

Correction: If someone in the group is being disruptive or you sense that they are speaking erroneously or on behalf of a spirit other than the Holy Spirit, then do to them as you would want done unto you. Keep the process as private as possible and avoid public humiliation. Do your best to maintain a heart of prayer for their good and the good of the group, even at the expense of your own ego. The point is to guard and protect everyone in the group (including them) from anything that could be damaging to their spiritual health and salvation. Follow Matthew 18 as a guideline for correcting error, as outlined below. Typically, the person will welcome correction and repent or leave on their own accord before you can see all of the steps through.

> ♦ Everybody can make a mistake once or twice or have a bad day. Therefore, before you initiate a corrective process it is best to wait and allow most errors pass uncorrected at least once or twice or until you are certain that there is a problem which threatens the spiritual health of the person or other members of the group. If they continue to repeat the disruption or error, proceed to the next step.

- If the person has been exceptionally disruptive or you are certain that the person is in error: Meet with them privately apart from the group meeting, gently point out their offense, and offer a correct approach. • Communicate clearly that this is the *first phase* of a corrective process, that they will receive one or two more warnings, and after that the group may be informed of their error and they may be asked to leave the group. If they continue to repeat the disruption or error, proceed to the next step.

- Meet with them again privately apart from the group meeting and have two or three others who are part of the group or have witnessed the erroneous behavior. Point out that their erroneous behavior has continued and offer a correct approach. • Communicate clearly that this is the *second phase* of a corrective process, that they will receive one *(or zero)* more warning and after that the group may be informed of their error and they may be asked to leave the group. • Repeat this step with the same two or three witnesses for as long as they seem to be sincerely repenting and receiving correction. Otherwise, proceed to next step, Option #1 or Option #2.

- Option #1: Inform the Group: Respectfully speak to the whole group about the situation. Treat it more like a family meeting than a crucifixion. • Communicate with consideration for the offender's dignity the type of disruptive or erroneous behavior that they have been engaging in. • Communicate clearly the steps of the corrective process above and how you have followed it. • Inform the group that the person will not be allowed to participate in ministry until the error has been corrected and that if they do, then they will be asked to leave the group. • Maintain an atmosphere of humility, mutual encouragement, grace, and growth for everyone.

- Option #2 – Ask Them to Leave: Privately and accompanied by the same two to three witnesses as before, communicate clearly that, until their error has been corrected, they are no longer welcome to participate in the group. • Offer them as much assistance as you can and try to point them in the direction of people or ministries that may be able to assist them. • Enforce the expulsion but always keep an eye out for signs of repentance.

- If the person repents, then welcome them back with complete forgiveness. Rejoice!

Manifestations of the Holy Spirit: I try to avoid the power of suggestion at all costs, so I will not articulate anything specific. This said, sometimes the power of God comes upon people in different ways or causes them to respond physically or emotionally. Sometimes, strange things happen that are completely the power of God at work and other times strange things happen that are not God at all.

When a person in your group or church experiences a physical or emotional manifestation, ask the Holy Spirit to give you discernment. Unless it is causing harm to the person or to others, allow it to pass the first time just in case it is God. If you sense that the person is re-creating a manifestation in their flesh or to get attention, then follow the steps for correction as outlined above. If you sense that the manifestation is demonic, then see *Activity 7: Cast Out Demons*.

Remember that Jesus functioned in more of God's power than any of us and He wasn't weird. He walked in peace, dignity, and majesty, He honored others above Himself, and loved everyone equally without partiality. We may be quirky and spastic at times along the way but Jesus is still our model of spiritual maturity and the One that we are called to be like.

Jealousy: Sometimes the people in our groups excel in certain spiritual gifts beyond where we are ourselves as their leader. Resist jealousy. See *Activity 2: Living Word* to remain in the love of Jesus for you or *Activity 5: Death to Life* to crucify your flesh and pride. Love is not jealous and where there is jealousy there is disorder and every evil thing.[3] You do not want this in your group and you certainly do not want to be the source of it. Do your best to love everyone whom God has given you to lead the way that Jesus loves you and leads you. Otherwise, you become less like Jesus and more like the ones who crucified Him.

My Prayer for Leaders

My prayer for you as leaders is that the members of your group will honor you with due respect and submit to you as you submit yourself to the Lord. May you pursue Christ in a way that they can follow you as you follow Him.

<hr />

[3] 1 Corinthians 13:4, James 3:16

INTRODCUTORY ACTIVITY
Cast Your Cares

Jesus set us free from sin and death so that we can live our lives unrestricted by worries and anxieties. In this Activity, we will list out our cares and burdens and hand them over to the Lord while trusting that He will take care of them for us.

This Activity will help you to:

- 🔥 Succinctly articulate the stresses of life that are weighing you down
- 🔥 Present your anxieties to God as an act of faith
- 🔥 Let go of your own will and way of doing things
- 🔥 Experience more freedom from fear, stress, and anxiety
- 🔥 Prepare yourself to receive revelation and instruction from God

Introduction: Cast Your Cares[4]

To a group of believers suffering intense hardship, the apostle Peter quoted Psalm 55 by saying, "Cast your cares upon the Lord because He cares for you." (see 1 Peter 5:7) The word *cast* in these passages means to *throw away, hurl, or place upon* and is the same word used for placing a load upon a donkey or beast of burden who carries the load while the person walks. In the same way, the Lord carries our worries, anxieties, and cares for us when we let Him. This is an act of humility, faith, and trust in God's faithfulness in caring about our cares and handling our problems. Usually, He takes care of our cares better than we do because His ways are so much higher than our ways.

Note: This Activity can be done before times of Bible study and prayer, before we start our day, or any time we feel anxious or worried about anything. By keeping our cares in God's hands, we are liberated to hear His voice and do what He says.

Step One: Prepare

Place a basket in the middle of the room or have a few people ready to walk around the room to collect the cares that group members are casting away.

Step Two: Identify

Take a moment to ponder the things that are weighing you down, troubling you, causing you to feel anxiety or frustration, or that you are worried about. Consider things that you need right now, relationships that are in distress, and situations that seem problematic.

---

[4] For more on casting your cares, see *ACTS, Introduction* and *Chapter 12: Devotion*

Step Three: Write

Try sum up each issue, need, or situation that you have identified with one word or a simple phrase. (i.e. "our marriage," "the mortgage payment," or "Mary.")

Write each short phrase expressing your cares, anxieties, worries, and frustrations on a slip of paper. ▪ Use one line for each care that you are casting on the Lord and use as many lines as you need. ▪ Resist the urge to give extensive details or to tell God how to handle the situation. God already knows what you mean and what you need. He has been God for a long time and He knows how to do His job.

Step Four: Cast Away

Say a quick prayer to God and believe in your heart that He will carry these burdens for you. It can be as simple as saying, *"God I trust that you care about my cares"* or *"Jesus, thank you for carrying my burdens for me."*

Crumple up the piece of paper with your cares written on it and throw it into a basket in the middle of the room or throw it away. Do this as an act of faith in the same way that you would throw a load onto a donkey or beast of burden. ▪ Trust that your cares are out of your hands and that God will take care of them because He cares for you.

Take a moment to experience the freedom of being burden-free by faith. ▪ Continue trusting that God is carrying your burden and resist the urge to resume carrying it yourself.

Step Five: Invite the Holy Spirit

Invite the Holy Spirit to come and to guide your study time, prayer time, or the rest of your day by simply saying, *"Come, Holy Spirit"* or *"Come, Lord Jesus."* ▪ Then, proceed into your time of study, prayer, or with the rest of your day with your ears open to whatever the Holy Spirit may want to speak to you.

Onward to Maturity:

Jesus came to set us free from all fear—even the fear of death. Return to this Activity any time you feel weighed down with fear, stress, or anxiety.

The aim of this activity is to be completely free from all fear, stress, and anxiety.

❧Additional Cast Your Cares Activation

Whenever anything is weighing you down or causing fear, stress, or anxiety, pray the way that Jesus taught His disciples to pray. ▪ Using the outline below as a guide for your prayers, pray out loud and from your heart with your present circumstances in mind. ▪ Invite the Holy Spirit to interrupt you and to minister to you as you go.

Thank God for being your heavenly Father. ▪ Take a moment ponder His goodness and His love for you.

Praise God that He is higher and more powerful than all other gods, idols, and the schemes of men. ▪ Praise God that everything in all creation must bow to the name of Jesus.

Ask for God's Kingdom to be established in your situation. ▪ Use the eyes of your heart to envision the way that things are in heaven. ▪ Ask for God's will to be done on earth as it is in heaven. ▪ Place your trust in God's ways instead of the ways of this world, the wisdom of man, or your own strength and abilities.

Ask God to supply all of your needs and trust that He will.

Admit any mistakes that you have made in bringing this situation upon yourself or aspects of the situation that you have handled poorly or handled in your own strength.

Forgive others who seem to be the perpetrators of your problems or who have offended you in any way.

Ask God to lead you in paths of righteousness and not into trials or temptations. ▪ Ask God to deliver you from evil. ▪ Trust that you are protected from harm by the blood of Jesus.

This then, is how you should pray:
Our Father in heaven,
Hallowed be your name,
Your Kingdom come, your will be done on earth as it is in heaven.
Give us this day our daily bread
And forgive us our trespasses
As we forgive those who trespass against us.
Lead us not into temptation but deliver us from evil.

ACTIVITY 1
Living the Gospel

We who believe that Jesus is Lord were included with Him in His crucifixion, death, resurrection, and ascension to heaven.[5] In this Activity, we will meditate on and identify ourselves with each aspect of the completed work of Christ's redemption so that we can be living demonstrations of the Gospel.

This Activity will help you to:

◊ Deepen your understanding Christ's sacrifice

◊ Let go of your own way of doing things

◊ Increase your ability to receive of the benefits of Christ's sacrifice

◊ Know your position as a child of God who is seated in Heaven

◊ Be completely free to obey the promptings of the Holy Spirit

Step One: Prepare the Room

Have everyone find their own comfortable place to sit, stand, or lay down within your meeting room. They may want to bring their Bible with them or bring a pen and paper in order to write down anything that the Lord may reveal to them during this time. ▪ Selected Scriptures are supplied on the Actsheet at the end of this chapter. (See also: www.activatedchurch.com/actsheets)

Designate one person to be the Leader of your time of meditation. The Leader is responsible for reading the instructions to the group and for transitioning the group from one phase of the meditation to the next.

Optional: If you desire to have worship music playing softly in the background, then begin playing the music and adjust the volume to a low setting so that everyone can hear the Leader over the sound of the music.

Note: Even though you are in the room together, this meditation is an opportunity for everyone to have a personal encounter with Jesus and the fullness of the Gospel. Therefore:

◊ Refrain from speaking or whispering to others during the meditation so that everyone can keep their attention focused on Jesus.

◊ If you see someone crying during the meditation time, leave them alone and let them cry. The Lord is most likely ministering to their heart in a powerful way.

◊ If you see someone that has fallen asleep, let them sleep until the meditation is completed. God does some of His best work when we rest deeply in Him.

◊ If you struggle with extended stillness, try to keep your mind focused on your love for Jesus.

---

[5] For an in-depth study on the Gospel of Jesus Christ, see *ACTS, Chapter 1: The Gospel*

Step Two: Prepare Your Hearts

⋄ Invite the Holy Spirit to come and to bless your time of meditation on the Gospel.

Ask the Holy Spirit to help you to see with the eyes of your heart and to experience each phase of the Gospel.

Open your hearts to receive everything that the Lord has for you during this time.

Step Three: The Cross

When Christ was crucified, we were crucified with Him. On the cross, all of our sins, our sinful nature, the curse of the Law, all of our sicknesses, pains, griefs, and the works of the devil waged war against Jesus and appeared to triumph.

In this phase of the meditation, imagine yourself on the cross with Christ. • Allow the Holy Spirit to bring to mind everything that is afflicting you right now. For example:

⋄ Things that you do or have done that you know are wrong
⋄ Your nature or aspects of yourself that are ungodly
⋄ Lack, defeat, subjugation to others, or inability to get ahead
⋄ Oppression from the evil one, torment, or compulsions
⋄ Sicknesses, pains, or griefs
⋄ Shame, humiliation, lack of dignity, or extreme vulnerability
⋄ This world and its demands for performance and money

Continue to envision yourself on the cross with Jesus in His crucifixion. • Allow the Holy Spirit to magnify your present afflictions even to the point of it appearing that your afflictions have triumphed over you.

Allow 2 to 3 minutes of stillness and silence or an appropriate amount of time for your group.

Leader: Alert the group that it is time to move into the next phase of the meditation.

Step Four: Death with Christ

When Christ died, His soul descended into darkness and we were included in His death with Him. In the stillness of death, every aspect of His and our humanity were terminated. Through death, the price for our sins was fully paid, the curse of the Law was broken, and our natural way of life was brought to an end.

In this phase of the meditation, imagine yourself in the stillness of death. • Make a concerted effort to release and let go of every affliction that was revealed in Step Two. • Believe in your heart that because you are dead, all of the charges of ungodliness against you fall to the ground so that there is no more need to fear God's punishment or even death. All of the rights of the evil one to oppress and torment you or to cause sickness, pain, and grief are rendered null and void. For example:

⋄ You are dead to all anxiety, guilt, fear, and shame.

⟡ You are dead to your own will and way of doing things.

⟡ You are dead to the Law of God and all attempts to earn God's favor.

⟡ You are dead to performance pressure and the ways of this world.

⟡ You are dead to all humiliation and offense.

⟡ You are dead to your own mind, will, and emotions.

⟡ You are dead to your own desires, plans, ambitions, and dreams.

Continue to envision yourself in the stillness of death. ▪ Allow the Holy Spirit to release you into total freedom from every affliction. ▪ Ask the Holy Spirit to give you deeper revelation of the fact that "It is finished!"

Allow 2 to 3 minutes of stillness and silence or an appropriate amount of time for your group.

Leader: Alert the group that it is time to move into the next phase of the meditation.

Step Five: Raised with Christ

When Christ was resurrected from the dead, we who believe were raised with Him. God breathed the breath of life into Jesus and He overcame death forever. Jesus was born again into resurrection life.

In this phase of the meditation, imagine yourself walking out of the grave as a new creation. ▪ Ask the Holy Spirit to breathe new life into you, to give you fresh hope, and to quicken your mortal body by God's power. ▪ Believe in your heart that everything about you has been made new in the resurrection life of Christ. For example:

⟡ You are alive and born again as a child of God with a living hope.

⟡ You are alive to the peace, wholeness, health, and provision of God.

⟡ You are alive in right standing with God in order to carry out His purposes.

⟡ You are alive to be led by the Holy Spirit in paths of righteousness.

⟡ You are alive to the supernatural and miraculous ways of God.

⟡ You are alive with the faith, hope, and love of Christ.

Continue to envision yourself in resurrection life. ▪ Ask the Holy Spirit to help you to understand that you now have right standing with God, as if you had never sinned. ▪ Offer yourself to Him as an instrument of righteousness.

Allow 2 to 3 minutes of stillness and silence or an appropriate amount of time for your group.

Leader: Alert the group that it is time to move into the next phase of the meditation.

Step Six: Ascended with Christ

When Christ ascended to heaven, we who believe ascended with Him to the right hand of the Father to be seated in heavenly places.

In this phase of the meditation, imagine yourself ascending into Heaven with Jesus. ▪ Ask the Holy Spirit to give you a vision of Heaven's throne room and to show you the way that things are in heaven. ▪ Envision yourself seated on the throne with Jesus.

Allow 2 to 3 minutes of stillness and silence or an appropriate amount of time for your group.

Leader: Alert the group that it is time to move into the next phase of the meditation.

Step Seven: Holy Spirit Poured Out

While we are spiritually seated in Christ in Heaven, our bodies remain on the earth. Therefore, after Christ ascended to heaven, He poured the Holy Spirit out to His disciples, giving us heaven's power so that we can be like Jesus and fulfill God's purposes.

In this phase of the meditation, ask God to pour out the Holy Spirit upon you. ▪ Have every person in the group say out loud, "Come Holy Spirit." ▪ Open your heart to receive the power of God in your inmost being. ▪ Ask for God's will to be done on earth as it is in heaven. ▪ Listen for anything that the Lord speaks to you during this time.

Allow 2 to 3 minutes of stillness and silence or an appropriate amount of time for your group.

Leader: Alert the group that the time of meditation is completed.

Step Eight: Share

Depending on the size of your group, partner up two-by-two, gather into small groups, or do this as one large group.

As you are comfortable doing so, share something new that God revealed to you by doing this Activity.

Onward to Maturity:

Disciples of Jesus are born again as children of God and new creations in Christ. Return to this Activity anytime you desire to experience the fullness of all that Christ did for us.

*The aim of this activity is to live as born again children of God
who have overcome the world, the flesh, and the devil.*

1 – *Living the Gospel - Actsheet*
SELECTED SCRIPTURES

I have been crucified with Christ and I no longer live, but Christ lives in me. The life I now live in the body, I live by faith in the Son of God, who loved me and gave himself for me. {Galatians 2:20}

For you died, and your life is now hidden with Christ in God. {Colossians 3:3}

Praise be to the God and Father of our Lord Jesus Christ, who has blessed us in the heavenly realms with every spiritual blessing in Christ. {Ephesians 1:3}

Your whole self ruled by the flesh was put off when you were circumcised by Christ, having been buried with him in baptism, in which you were also raised with him through your faith in the working of God, who raised him from the dead. {Colossians 2:11-12}

For we know that our old self was crucified with him so that the body ruled by sin might be done away with, that we should no longer be slaves to sin. {Romans 6:6}

Christ redeemed us from the curse of the law by becoming a curse for us, for it is written: "Cursed is everyone who is hung on a pole." {Galatians 3:13}

Once you were alienated from God and were enemies in your minds because of your evil behavior. But now he has reconciled you by Christ's physical body through death to present you holy in his sight, without blemish and free from accusation. {Colossians 1:21-22}

We were therefore buried with him through baptism into death in order that, just as Christ was raised from the dead through the glory of the Father, we too may live a new life... For we know that since Christ was raised from the dead, he cannot die again; death no longer has mastery over him. The death he died, he died to sin once for all; but the life he lives, he lives to God. In the same way, count yourselves dead to sin but alive to God in Christ Jesus. Therefore do not let sin reign in your mortal body so that you obey its evil desires. Do not offer any part of yourself to sin as an instrument of wickedness, but rather offer yourselves to God as those who have been brought from death to life; and offer every part of yourself to him as an instrument of righteousness. {Romans 6:4, 9-13}

But because of his great love for us, God, who is rich in mercy, made us alive with Christ even when we were dead in transgressions--it is by grace you have been saved. And God raised us up with Christ and seated us with him in the heavenly realms in Christ Jesus. {Ephesians 2:4-6}

Praise be to the God and Father of our Lord Jesus Christ! In his great mercy he has given us new birth into a living hope through the resurrection of Jesus Christ from the dead, and into an inheritance that can never perish, spoil or fade. {1 Peter 1:3-4}

Therefore, if anyone is in Christ, the new creation has come: The old has gone, the new is here! {2 Corinthians 5:17}

ACTIVITY 2
Living Word

God speaks to us through His Word with love and wisdom for our lives today. When we honor and approach the Scriptures as the Living Word of God, the Holy Spirit is free to speak directly into our lives so that we are strengthened to know God's will and to do it. In this Activity, we will engage with God through *lectio divina*, or *divine reading* of the Scriptures.

This Activity will help you to:

◊ Listen to God speak to you through the Scriptures
◊ Deepen your understanding of God's will for you
◊ Hear the promptings of the Holy Spirit for your life today
◊ Let go of your own will and way of doing things
◊ Become more confident in doing the will of the Father

Introduction: Lectio Divina (Divine Reading)

The origins of *lectio divina* date back to Christian monks who meditated on the Word of God as an act of devotion. These monks sought to commune with God through the Scriptures in order to receive divine inspiration rather than theological knowledge. This practice engages with the Word of God in a way that is personal, relevant, and applicable.

Step One: 1ˢᵗ Reading *(Lectio)*

◊ Before the first reading, allow for a moment of stillness and silence. ▪ Invite the Holy Spirit to come.

Have one person in your group read John 15:1-11 out loud at a slow pace. (Additional passages can be found at the end of this chapter.) ▪ As the reader reads, open your spiritual ears to hear one word or phrase from the passage that stands out to you or seems to linger in your ear.

After the reading is completed, write down the word or phrase that caught your attention on a piece of paper. ▪ Alternatively, if your group is comfortable doing so, speak the word or phrase out loud.

Allow several moments of silence in the presence of God. ▪ Listen to what the Holy Spirit is speaking to you through the word or phrase. ▪ Resist analyzing, intellectualizing, or trying to figure it out. Let the Holy Spirit do the talking and write down your impressions of what the Holy Spirit is saying to you.

Step Two: 2ⁿᵈ Reading *(Meditatio)*

Read the same passage out loud a second time and at a slow pace. (You may consider having a different person do the second reading.) ▪ This time, open your ears to hear what God is speaking directly into your life today through this passage. Is He extending an invitation to you? Speaking of His love for you?

Asking you to trust Him? Instructing you to do something or to wait?

After the second reading is completed, allow several moments of silence in the presence of God. ▪ Listen again to what the Holy Spirit is speaking to you. ▪ Resist the urge to converse with God. Let the Holy Spirit do the talking and write down your impressions of what the Holy Spirit is saying to you.

Step Three: 3rd Reading (*Oratio*)

Read the same passage out loud a third time and at a slow pace. (You may consider having yet another person do the third reading.)

After the third reading is complete, talk to God in silent prayer. Respond to what God has revealed or spoken to you. ▪ Resist the urge to feign an appropriate answer to what God has said. Be as honest with God as you possibly can be about your genuine response to what the Holy Spirit has revealed. ▪ Tell Him openly about any resistance or fear you have, or any barriers that you perceive are blocking you. Or, share with Him the love or joy you feel in your heart at His invitation to intimacy with Him or for the wisdom that He has given you today.

Allow time for the Holy Spirit to respond to what you are saying. ▪ Remember that conversations are two-way with both parties having the opportunity to speak.

Step Four: Contemplate (*Contemplatio*)

After your prayer time is completed, allow for several moments of silence in the presence of God. ▪ Allow what the Holy Spirit has spoken to you to penetrate deeply into your heart. ▪ Release the areas of resistance and surrender yourself more deeply to God. ▪ Commit yourself to following through with the instructions that God speaks to you during this time.

Ask the Holy Spirit to give you one word or phrase that will help you to remember throughout your day what God has revealed in this time of devotion.

Onward to Maturity:

Return to this Activity anytime you need to hear the Holy Spirit speak directly into your life or to deepen your intimacy with God. This Activity can be done using almost any Scripture passage. In addition to John 15:1-11 as mentioned above, recommended passages include:

Psalm 1	Mark 10:46-52	John 6:25-34	Hebrews 4:9-13
Proverbs 8:1-11	1 Corinthians 13:4-13	John 10:1-15	2 Peter 1:3-11
Mark 4:26-29	Luke 1:26-38	Romans 8:1-11	Psalm 27
Psalm 23	Luke 10:38-42	Colossians 2:6-15	1 Corinthians 2:9-16

The aim of this activity is to hear the voice of God and do what He says.

ACTIVITY 3
Communion

Jesus Christ paid for us to be set free from sin and every form of bondage and oppression through the sacrifice of His body and the shedding of His blood. In His resurrection, we who believe were raised with Him as a new covenant people of God who have been freed from death and the clutches of the evil one. In this Activity, we will renew our understanding of Christ's body and His blood, test the genuineness of our faith, and partake of the life of God as His Church.

This Activity will help you to:

- ♦ Deepen your understanding Christ's sacrifice
- ♦ Test and affirm your faith
- ♦ Increase your ability to receive of the benefits of Christ's sacrifice
- ♦ Receive the life of God in your inmost being
- ♦ Build your identity as a member of the Church, the Body of Christ

Introduction: Communion[6]

On the night of the first Passover, God's people painted the blood of the lamb on the doorposts of their homes as an act of faith by which God protected them from the destroyer. On the third day, God supernaturally delivered the newborn nation of Israel from oppressive slavery in Egypt by walking them through the parted waters of the Red Sea so that they were free to worship Him. Since then, every time that Jews have celebrated Passover, they have commemorated how God moved so mightily on their behalf as His people.

For Christians today, Jesus Christ is our eternal Passover Lamb who takes away the sins of the world (see John 1:29; 1 Corinthians 5:7) Jesus' blood was shed for the forgiveness of our sins so that we can be protected from the destruction of sin and the evil one. His body was broken so that we can freely enter into the presence of God to worship. On the third day, when God raised Jesus from the dead, the Church was born as a new covenant people who will worship God for eternity. We partake of communion to commemorate Christ's sacrifice, to continually renew our faith in what was accomplished for us through His death and resurrection, and to look forward to His return.

The earliest disciples of Christ shared communion or "broke bread" whenever they met together. Communion bread and wine were made readily available for them to serve themselves and to serve one another. As a holy nation and a royal priesthood, (1 Peter 2:9) every believer is a priest of God and able to administer the body and blood of Christ with due reverence. This said, communion and the benefits of

---

[6] For an in-depth teaching on Communion, see *ACTS, Chapter 3: Communion*

Christ's sacrifice are only available to those who believe that Jesus is Lord and that God raised Him from the dead. Unbelievers should abstain from communion or, better yet, believe Jesus and partake.

Step One: Prepare the Bread and the Wine

Acquire bread and wine (or juice) to be consecrated to God for the purpose of Communion.

Bread: My personal preference is to use unleavened bread. This is because yeast is symbolic of sin and, therefore, I believe that communion bread without yeast properly represents that Jesus was without sin. Also, unleavened bread symbolized that the Israelites were ready to depart in haste and, therefore, it serves to remind us as believers to be ready for our departure from this world at Christ's return. ▪ Unleavened bread can be purchased at the store around Passover time or made from simple ingredients. As an alternative, matzos crackers (even if they are marked "Not for Passover") or any kind of flat cracker or wafer can be used. If none of these are readily available, regular bread is acceptable.

Wine/Juice: My personal preference is to use real wine even though I do not otherwise drink alcohol. For me, there is something about the bitterness of real wine with communion that adds impact to the remembrance of Christ's suffering. You could even say that the bitterness makes it sweeter. ▪ For those who are completely opposed the consumption of alcohol, grape juice is a good alternative. ▪ If you decide to use real wine, it is wise to supply both wine and juice in order to allow people to choose and not cause offense.

Consecrate: Once you have the bread and wine/juice, pray over them and devote them exclusively to the purpose of Communion. It can be as simple as, *"In the name of Jesus I consecrate this bread and this wine/juice to God's service and for the purpose of communion."* ▪ As you pray, believe in your heart that the bread and wine/juice are made holy by your prayer. ▪ Set them aside in a special place and do not use them for regular snacking or cooking.

Service: Decide in advance how best to distribute the body and blood of Jesus to the group so that everyone is able to partake of communion within your allotted time. ▪ I prefer to break the bread during the communion service or have each person break off their own piece of bread, but the bread can also be broken into pieces in advance. ▪ I prefer to use individual-sized disposable communion cups for the wine/juice. These can be purchased inexpensively. Otherwise, any small cups will suffice.

Step Two: Perceive the Body and the Blood

When Jesus was still alive, He demonstrated the act of communion to His disciples by saying, "This *is* my body" and, "This *is* my blood" (emphasis added) even though His body had not yet been broken and His blood had not yet been shed. (see Matthew 26:26-29; Mark 14:22-25; Luke 22:14-20; John 13:21-30) He did not say that it *becomes* or that it *represents*, He said it *is*. Therefore, we partake of communion by faith that the bread *is* His body and the wine/juice *is* His blood.

Wait for everyone to be present. ▪ Bring the consecrated bread and wine/juice into plain view.

◊ Invite the Holy Spirit to come and say a quick prayer for your time of communion together.

Find the *Body and Blood of Jesus* Actsheet supplied at the end of this chapter. (See also: www.activatedchurch.com/actsheets) Designate one person to read the Scriptures or decide to rotate around the group with each person reading one Scripture at a time. ▪ Read the *Body and Blood of Jesus* Scriptures out loud at a slow pace. ▪ As the Scriptures are read out loud, focus your attention on the bread and wine/juice. ▪ Believe in your heart that the Scriptures apply to the bread and wine/juice that you are about to eat and drink.

Step Three: Examine Yourself

As believers, we must examine ourselves before partaking of communion in order to test the genuineness of our faith in all that Christ has done for us. Without genuine faith and reverence, we drink judgment upon ourselves. This can be the cause of weakness, illness, and even death. (see 1 Corinthians 11:27-31)

Have someone in the group read the following questions out loud. ▪ As these questions are read, allow the Holy Spirit to examine the genuineness of your faith. ▪ Answer these questions silently in your heart:

- Do you believe that Jesus Christ shed His blood for the forgiveness of your sins?
- Do you believe that you are totally and completely forgiven?
- Do you believe that you can receive all of the benefits of Christ's body and blood (according to the Scriptures) as a free gift of grace through faith in Jesus?
- Do you regard the communion bread and wine/juice as holy and consecrated to God?

Allow for a moment of stillness and silence for self-examination. ▪ If your answer to all of these questions is *yes*, then allow the Holy Spirit to highlight any particular aspect of the benefits of communion for you to receive more fully today. ▪ If your answer to any of these questions is *no*, then consider abstaining from communion today.

Note: Sin in your life is NOT a reason to abstain from partaking of communion. In fact, the forgiveness of your sins is one of the primary purposes of Christ's sacrifice. ▪ If you feel burdened by sin, confess it to God sincerely from your heart. ▪ Partake of communion and receive God's forgiveness as a free gift. ▪ Then, go and sin no more.

Step Four: Remember and Proclaim the Lord's Death

Read the following passage out loud:

> *The Lord Jesus on the night when he was betrayed took bread, and when he had given thanks, he broke it, and said, "This is my body which is for you. Do this in remembrance of me." In the same way also he took the cup, after supper, saying, "This cup is the new covenant in my blood. Do this, as often as you drink it, in remembrance of me." For as often as you eat this bread and drink the cup, you proclaim the Lord's death until he comes. (1 Corinthians 11:23-26)*

As the reader reads, remember in your heart Jesus' sacrificial death and resurrection or the story of your own salvation when you first believed that Jesus is Lord.

Praise God that because of Jesus' sacrifice, you are protected from the Destroyer until Jesus returns to reign for all eternity.

Step Five: Partake

Take a moment to look around the room at the people of God. As Christians, we are one nation, one people, one family, one body. Acknowledge in your heart that all believers are children of God and your brothers and sisters in Christ. • Do not reproach anyone who has decided to abstain from communion.

As you eat the bread and drink the wine/juice, be consciously strengthened with the life and power of God in your inmost being. The indestructible life of Christ and the same power that raised Christ from the dead is in us to give life to our bodies, strengthen us in our trials, and enable us to work miracles, signs, and wonders in the earth.

◊ Approach #1: Led in Unison

Designate one person to lead the group in communion. This person is the Leader. • If you have not already done so, distribute the body and the blood of Jesus to everyone who is partaking of communion today. • Do not eat or drink until everyone has received the bread and wine/juice.

Leader: Say out loud, "This is the body of Christ which was broken for you." • Then, everyone eat the body of Christ at the same time.

Leader: Say out loud, "This is the blood of Jesus which was shed for the forgiveness of your sins." • Then, everyone drink the blood of Jesus at the same time.

◊ Approach #2: Serve One Another

Designate one believer to be the first to serve communion. This believer is the Server. • Have the Server bring the body and blood to another believer. This believer is the Recipient.

Server: Ask for the Recipient's first name if you do not already know it. Look into their eyes as you serve them.

Server: Allow the Recipient to take a piece of bread. • As they take the body of Christ, say, "[Their name], this is the body of Christ which was broken for you." • Then, give them time to eat the body of Christ.

Server: Allow the Recipient to take a cup of wine/juice. • As they take the blood of Jesus, say, "[Their name], this is the blood of Jesus which was shed for the forgiveness of your sins." • Then, allow them to drink the blood of Jesus.

Server: Transfer the bread and wine/juice to the Recipient so that they become the next Server.

Recipient: You have now become the Server. Carry the body and blood of Jesus to another believer as the next Recipient and follow the steps given above for the Server.

Repeat the steps above until every believer in the room has been served. • Note: The first person to be the Server will most likely be the last person to be the Recipient.

Step Six: Worship

After every believer has been served, take a moment to praise and worship God. Share what is on your heart about God's goodness and love. Enjoy fellowship with one another as the people of God.

Step Seven: Devote or Destroy

Anything consecrated to the Lord is devoted for a special purpose and if it will not be used for this purpose, it must be destroyed. ▪ If you will be serving communion again soon, then set the bread and wine apart for this special purpose and do not use it for anything else. ▪ If you will not be serving communion again soon, then throw the bread away and pour the wine/juice down the drain. Any other use is dishonoring the body and blood of the Lord and may cause weakness, illness, or death.

Onward to Maturity:

Communion is a very special way of participating in the life of God as His sons and daughters. Take communion any time you need to remember and receive all that God has done for you as a free gift through the sacrificial death and resurrection of Jesus. Take communion any time you need to unite with other believers or be at peace with one another.

The aim of this activity is to dynamically receive the benefits of Christ's sacrifice while becoming one with God and with one another.

3 – *Communion - Actsheet*
BODY AND BLOOD OF JESUS

Selection of Scriptures

Jesus said to them, "Very truly I tell you, unless you eat the flesh of the Son of Man and drink his blood, you have no life in you. Whoever eats my flesh and drinks my blood has eternal life, and I will raise them up at the last day. For my flesh is real food and my blood is real drink. Whoever eats my flesh and drinks my blood remains in me, and I in them. Just as the living Father sent me and I live because of the Father, so the one who feeds on me will live because of me. {John 6:53-57}

THE BODY OF CHRIST

We have been made holy through the sacrifice of the body of Jesus Christ once for all. {Hebrews 10:10}

But now he has reconciled you by Christ's physical body through death to present you holy in his sight, without blemish and free from accusation. {Colossians 1:22}

"He himself bore our sins" in his body on the cross, so that we might die to sins and live for righteousness; "by his wounds you have been healed." {1Peter 2:24}

THE BLOOD OF JESUS

In him we have redemption through his blood, the forgiveness of sins, in accordance with the riches of God's grace. {Ephesians 1:7}

Since we have now been justified by his blood, how much more shall we be saved from God's wrath through him! {Romans 5:9}

Therefore, brothers and sisters, since we have confidence to enter the Most Holy Place by the blood of Jesus, {Hebrews 10:19}

And so Jesus also suffered outside the city gate to make the people holy through his own blood. {Hebrews 13:12}

How much more, then, will the blood of Christ, who through the eternal Spirit offered himself unblemished to God, cleanse our consciences from acts that lead to death, so that we may serve the living God! {Hebrews 9:14}

But if we walk in the light, as he is in the light, we have fellowship with one another, and the blood of Jesus, his Son, purifies us from all sin. {1Johon 1:7}

And they sang a new song, saying: "You are worthy to take the scroll and to open its seals, because you were slain, and with your blood you purchased for God persons from every tribe and language and people and nation. {Revelation 5:9}

They triumphed over him by the blood of the Lamb and by the word of their testimony; they did not love their lives so much as to shrink from death. {Revelation 12:11}

ACTIVITY 4
Remember His Love

God's love for us is revealed in memorable ways when He intervenes in our lives for our good. By remembering the times that God has worked on our behalf, we are encouraged to trust His love and faithfulness toward us in our present trials. In this Activity, we will look back at episodes from our personal history with God in order to renew our trust in Him for the trials that we face today.

This Activity will help you to:

- Build a record of God's faithfulness towards you
- Increase your faith for the trials that you face today
- Attain more and more freedom from fear
- Become more certain of God's ongoing and unconditional love toward you

Introduction: Remembering God's Love – Psalm 136

Psalm 136 recounts the history of God's love toward His people, Israel. Every verse includes an instance of God's faithfulness followed by the phrase, "His love endures forever." In times of trial and distress, this psalm was most likely read by the whole congregation. The priest would read the example of God's intervention in the past and the people would respond with praise that, "His love endures forever!" Remembering God's mighty deeds from their history built up their faith as they encountered new adversaries.

As an example, in the days of King Jehoshaphat, Judah was surrounded by a great multitude of enemies. Jehoshaphat assembled everyone together to worship the Lord in this way, remembering His mighty deeds and saying, "His love endures forever!" While they worshipped and rested in God's faithfulness, God moved miraculously on their behalf. (see 2 Chronicles 20)

Step One: Your History with God

Recall the times that God has been faithful in your life. • Start with the story of your salvation. What did God rescue you from? What was your life like then? What path of life were you on? How did God rescue you from darkness and destruction? • Then, progress through your history with God. What are the other times that God has rescued you? Saved you from harm or from yourself? Given you something you did not deserve? Moved powerfully on your behalf?

Step Two: Write Your Own Psalm 136

Use the *My Own Psalm 136* Actsheet at the end of this chapter as an example or use a separate piece of paper to write your own Psalm 136. (See also: www.activatedchurch.com/actsheets) • Write the stories of

God's love and faithfulness toward you in the blank spaces between "His steadfast love endures forever."

Once you have finished writing, pause for a moment. • Then, read the history of God's faithfulness to you, taking time to include "His love endures forever." • Meditate on all that He has done for you and ponder the ways that He has blessed you.

Step Three: Today's Trials

Moving into the present, consider the trials that are impacting your life right now. • Talk to God about any difficulties that you are having as you believe Him in your current situation. Tell Him why this seems different to you or why it is particularly hard for you to trust and believe Him in this trial. • Talk to God about objections or resistances voiced by your intellect, flesh, religion, or pride and any areas where you feel guilt, shame, or fear. • Allow the Holy Spirit to speak to you and minister to you in these areas.

Ask God to give you wisdom for how to handle the trials in your life today. • If you hear a directive word from the Lord, commit yourself to obeying what He has instructed you to do. • If you do not hear a directive word about your current situation, believe that God will give you wisdom in the course of time.

Praise God for His love and faithfulness toward you in times past. • Reaffirm your faith in God and His ways for your present trials.

Onward to Maturity:

As you continue to walk with God, keep your personal Psalm 136 up to date. When you experience God's love and faithfulness toward you, add it to your Psalm 136. When trials come, return to your Psalm 136 to meditate on God's mighty works and reaffirm your faith in Him and His ways.

The aim of this activity is to live by faith in God and endure victoriously through every trial.

4 – *Remember His Love* - Actsheet
MY OWN PSALM 136

His Love Endures Forever

Give thanks to the LORD, for he is good,

> *for his steadfast love endures forever.*

to him who alone does great wonders,

> *for his steadfast love endures forever.*

Your history: _____

> *for his steadfast love endures forever.*

Your history: _____

> *for his steadfast love endures forever.*

Your history: _____

> *for his steadfast love endures forever.*

Your history: _____

> *for his steadfast love endures forever.*

Your history: _____

> *for his steadfast love endures forever.*

Your history: _____

> *for his steadfast love endures forever.*

Your history: _____

> *for his steadfast love endures forever.*

Your history: _____

> *for his steadfast love endures forever.*

It is he who remembered us in our low estate

> *for his steadfast love endures forever.*

and rescued us from our foes,

> *for his steadfast love endures forever.*

Give thanks to the God of heaven,

> *for his steadfast love endures forever.*

♦ Additional Remember His Love Activation

As we walk through life with the Lord, it is common for us to begin to consider that our salvation, healing, deliverance, or sustenance is somehow dependent on our actions rather than on the finished work of Jesus. This is why the New Testament is full of adjurations to believers to remember the simplicity of devotion Christ and the way that we learned Christ at first.

The Way That You Learned Christ

How did you first learn Christ? Write down the story of your salvation or ponder it in your heart. What did you do? What did He do? How did you know Him in your heart? • Consider the condition that you were in when you first believed and answer the following questions:

> ♦ Did Jesus save you because you were a good person? Were you better than other people?
> ♦ Had you earned His love in any way?
> ♦ Had you obeyed the law and been perfectly righteous?
> ♦ Had you practiced steps, techniques, or spiritual principles to effect your salvation?
> ♦ Was it because of your great faith or your perfect prayers?
> ♦ Was it because of your knowledge of the Scriptures?
> ♦ Was it because of your great wisdom, hard work, or success?
> ♦ Was it because you were trusting in common sense, your own strength, or other people?
> ♦ Had you done anything at all to deserve to be saved?

Consider your present circumstances and the trials that you are enduring. What are you placing your faith in or what do you believe that you are doing that is able to effectuate God's will in your life? • Review the list above to determine if you are placing your faith in something other than God's free gift of grace through Jesus Christ.

Admit to God the ways that you have been placing faith in your own efforts and let go of self-righteousness, legalism, and striving to earn God's love and blessing.

Open your heart to receive God's love and blessing as a free and unmerited gift of grace through faith in Jesus Christ. Wait and watch what God does in His time and in His way.

♦

ACTIVITY 5
Death to Life

In Christ, we have been set free and born again so that we can hear and obey the voice of God. In this Activity, we will uncover areas where our old nature of Adam, sin, the curse of the Law, and the Kingdom of Darkness have been hindering our ability to receive the fullness of Christ's finished work. By identifying ourselves in Christ's crucifixion, we will reckon all of these areas of limitation to be dead, causing their impact on our lives to be null and void. Then, we will move through the transfer from death to new life as a child of God who lives by the promptings of the Holy Spirit.

This Activity will help you to:

⟑ Attain a clear conscience through the blood of Jesus

⟑ Increase your discernment of good and evil

⟑ Remove limitations on your ability to receive blessing

⟑ Receive your identity as a born again child of God

⟑ Become free to do the will of the Father

This Activity utilizes several Actsheets. See www.activatedchurch.com/actsheets for printable pdf files.

Step One: Identifying the Old Man

⟑ Invite the Holy Spirit to come and guide your time. Ask the Holy Spirit to examine your heart and to help you to identify things that you believe have or could hold you back from being loved or blessed by God, receive any of God's benefits, or be used by God for ministry to others.

Find the Death to Life Actsheet #1, *The Old Man*. ▪ Ask the Holy Spirit to reveal one category from the "Old Man" column for you to focus on. It will be the one category that seems to draw you in or that "pops" off the page more than the others.

Within the category that the Holy Spirit has highlighted for you, read the "Examples" column. ▪ On a separate piece of paper, write down the things in this category that resonate with you the most. ▪ Ask and allow the Holy Spirit to reveal anything else from your life that fits in this category but is not specifically listed.

Step Two: It is Finished, Part One

Find the Death to Life Actsheet #2, *It is Finished*.

Within the category that the Holy Spirit has revealed to you, read through the Scriptures on the *It is Finished* Actsheet. ▪ Note that the scriptures given are in the **past tense** as things that have **already been done.**

Allow a moment of stillness and silence as you meditate on the Scriptures. ▪ Ask the Holy Spirit to give you deeper revelation of your inclusion in Christ's crucifixion and death.

Step Three: Crucified with Christ

Find the Death to Life Actsheet #3, *Crucified with Christ.*

Engage your mind, will, and emotions and follow the instructions within your focus category on the *Crucified with Christ* Actsheet. ▪ Commit to doing these things as an act of faith in your heart and ask the Holy Spirit to help you.

Allow several moments of stillness and silence. ▪ Talk to God about any objections or resistances voiced by your intellect, flesh, religion, or pride. ▪ Talk to God about any areas where you still feel guilt, shame, condemnation, or fear. ▪ Allow the Holy Spirit to speak to you and minister to you in these areas.

Step Four: Freedom through Death in Christ

Find the Death to Life Actsheet #4, *Dead in Christ.*

Partner with one other person. ▪ One person is the Recipient and the other person is the Minister.

Recipient: Share with your partner the category that the Holy Spirit revealed to you. ▪ If you are comfortable doing so, share the examples within this category that are impacting your life. ▪ If you are comfortable doing so, share the internal objections you are encountering on your path to receiving full freedom. ▪ As you receive ministry from your partner, believe in your heart that Christ conquered all of these things for you through His sacrifice.

Minister: Using the the *Dead in Christ* Actsheet, within the Recipient's focus category, speak the commands given in the "Command Freedom in Christ" column as a guideline to set your partner free. ▪ As you speak the commands to them, believe in your heart that Christ conquered all of these things for them through His sacrifice. ▪ As you minster to your partner, listen for promptings from the Holy Spirit for anything else that the Lord may want to speak to them and share it with them for prayerful consideration.

Change roles so that the Minister is now the Recipient. ▪ Repeat this step so that both of you minister and receive ministry from one another.

Step Five: It is Finished, Part Two

Return to the Death to Life Actsheet #2, *It is Finished*.

On the *It is Finished* Actsheet, read the Scriptures in the "New Life" category at the bottom of the page.

Allow several moments of stillness and silence as you meditate on your new life in Christ. ▪ Ask the Holy Spirit to give you deeper revelation of the change that took place when you believed Jesus and were transferred from death to life. ▪ Focus your heart on receiving the fullness of Christ's redemption.

Step Six: Raised with Christ

Find the Death to Life Actsheet #5, *Raised with Christ.*

Return your attention to your partner. • Using the *Raised with Christ* Actsheet, take turns as the Recipient and Minister, speaking the commands and statements in the "New Creation" category to one another. • As you give and receive ministry with one another, believe in your hearts the words that you are speaking and hearing.

Step Seven: Totally Cleansed

Allow several moments of stillness and silence. • Ask the Holy Spirit to help you to see with the eyes of your heart. Envision the old you and everything you have done being completely washed off of you. • If you have been water baptized, remember your own baptism and recognize with new clarity that the transfer from old to new took place as you submerged under the water and came up as a new creation. • Envision yourself as one who is completely clean and dressed in white linen.

Talk to God about anything prohibiting your conscience from being totally cleansed. • Allow the Holy Spirit to speak to you and minister to you in these areas.

Step Eight: Pray

Return your attention to your partner. • If you are comfortable doing so, share with one another any remaining resistances or unbelief. • Repeat the commands from Steps Three and Four as needed.

Use the prayers in the "Child of God" category on the *Raised with Christ* Actsheet as a guideline to pray for one another for the Father's guidance and direction. • Listen for promptings from the Holy Spirit and share with one another your impressions of what the Holy Spirit may be saying.

Onward to Maturity:

As the Holy Spirit leads you, repeat this Activity for all the other categories. As you walk with God and grow in Christlikeness, return to this Activity when perceived limitation, unbelief, guilt, shame, oppression, or pride seem to be blocking your way to receiving the love of the Father or to obeying the promptings of the Holy Spirit.

The aim of this activity is to be absolutely surrendered to the will of God and completely free from all fear.

5 – Death to Life – Actsheet #1
THE OLD MAN

Old Man	Examples
Nature of Sin Descended from Adam	◊ Anything that you were born with or into. ◊ Race, gender, genes, height, age… ◊ Generational curses, family patterns of behavior… ◊ Heritage, nationality, region, tribe… ◊ Sensual mind, depravity, futile thinking, vanity, hardness of heart, selfishness, narcissism…
Acts of Sin Trespasses Iniquities	◊ Anything done by you, including your thoughts and motives. ◊ Lying, cheating, moral failures, errors, accidents, behavioral patterns, habits, addictions… ◊ Evil desires, pride, competition, slander, covetousness, obscene talk, hatred, the way you have treated others, murder… ◊ Sexual immorality, impurity, lust…
Curse of the Law Afflictions Oppressions	◊ Any limitation on your ability to receive blessing. ◊ Lack, defeat, missed opportunities, inability to get ahead, lack of joy… ◊ Sickness, physical limitations, weakness, miscarriages, stillbirths… ◊ Subjugation to others, broken relationships, self-loathing…
Kingdom of Darkness False Spirituality Religion	◊ Any involvement that you have had with works of the devil. ◊ All forms of spirituality not rooted in Christ, occult involvement, divination, consulting the dead, idol worship, man worship… ◊ Fortunes told to you or about you, spoken curses, spells, witchcraft, unwise vows… ◊ Religious piety, asceticism, ordinances of man, philosophy, tradition, legalism… ◊ Elementary principles of nature or this world, astrology, horoscopes, karma…
Personal Attributes Advantages Disadvantages	◊ Anything that you have going for you or against you. ◊ Skills, birthrights, history of experiences, status, wealth/poverty, what you are known for, marriage/singleness/divorce, location… ◊ Successes/failures, education level, physical abilities/limitations, looks/appearance… ◊ The way that you were raised, the way that others have treated you, the lifestyle that you are accustomed to…

We have been crucified, forgiven, redeemed, transferred, and delivered by the blood of Jesus.

5 – Death to Life – Actsheet #2
IT IS FINISHED

Old Man	Selection of Scriptures
Nature of Sin	I have been crucified with Christ and I no longer live, but Christ lives in me. The life I now live in the body, I live by faith in the Son of God, who loved me and gave himself for me. {Galatians 2:20} For we know that our old self was crucified with him so that the body ruled by sin might be done away with, that we should no longer be slaves to sin-- {Romans 6:6}
Acts of Sin	Once you were alienated from God and were enemies in your minds because of your evil behavior. But now he has reconciled you by Christ's physical body through death to present you holy in his sight, without blemish and free from accusation {Colossians 1:21-22} In him we have redemption through his blood, the forgiveness of sins, in accordance with the riches of God's grace {Ephesians 1:7}
Curse of the Law	Christ redeemed us from the curse of the law by becoming a curse for us, for it is written: "Cursed is everyone who is hung on a pole." {Galatians 3:13}
Kingdom of Darkness	For he has rescued us from the dominion of darkness and brought us into the kingdom of the Son he loves, {Colossians 1:13} [Christ is] far above all rule and authority, power and dominion, and every name that is invoked, not only in the present age but also in the one to come. {Ephesians 1:21}
Personal Attributes	But God chose the foolish things of the world to shame the wise; God chose the weak things of the world to shame the strong. God chose the lowly things of this world and the despised things-and the things that are not-to nullify the things that are, so that no one may boast before him. {1 Corinthians 1:27-29} May I never boast except in the cross of our Lord Jesus Christ, through which the world has been crucified to me, and I to the world. {Galatians 6:14}
New Life	Your whole self ruled by the flesh was put off when you were circumcised by Christ, having been buried with him in baptism, in which you were also raised with him through your faith in the working of God, who raised him from the dead. {Colossians 2:11-12} We were therefore buried with him through baptism into death in order that, just as Christ was raised from the dead through the glory of the Father, we too may live a new life. {Romans 6:4}

5 – *Death to Life – Actsheet #3*
CRUCIFIED WITH CHRIST

Old Man	Reckon Your Old Self Dead
Nature of Sin	♦ Reckon yourself dead. ♦ Put to death the need to be right or to be recognized for what you do. ♦ Surrender your desires to God. Dead people do not have desires. ♦ Surrender your ways of doing thing and "the way that we have always done it." ♦ Stop regarding anything about what you were born into as a limitation on God's ability to use you.
Acts of Sin	♦ By grace through faith, receive forgiveness as a free gift because of Jesus' sacrifice. ♦ Believe that your errors, faults, failures, and the punishment for them have been canceled at the cross. ♦ Regard guilt, shame, fear, and remembrance of sin as an attack of the enemy. ♦ Stop defending yourself. Let God defend you.
Curse of the Law	♦ Recognize areas of oppression, affliction, or subjugation in your life. Believe that God paid for those areas to be blessed through the blood of Jesus. ♦ By grace through faith, receive the blessing of your full inheritance in Christ.
Kingdom of Darkness	♦ Renounce forever all involvement with all forms of false spirituality and believe that the blood of Jesus protects you from its effects. ♦ Stop doing anything from a motive of earning favor with God. Believe that Jesus fulfilled every religious act for you. ♦ Stop believing that the ways of this world dictate the path of your life. ♦ Regard guilt, shame, condemnation, and fear as an attack of the enemy.
Personal Attributes	♦ Stop placing confidence in anything that you have regarded as a personal advantage. Trust God. ♦ Stop believing that anything which you have regarded as a disadvantage in your life has any power to prevent God from blessing you or using you. Trust God.

We have been crucified, forgiven, redeemed, transferred, and delivered by the blood of Jesus.

5 – Death to Life – Actsheet #4
DEAD IN CHRIST

Old Man	Command Freedom in Christ
Nature of Sin	♦ In the power and authority of the name of Jesus, I command the nature of Adam and sin in you to be dead. ♦ In the name of Jesus, I command your flesh into subjection to Christ. I take authority over your flesh and command the members of your body and it's desires to be silent. ♦ In the power and authority of the name of Jesus, I break all generational curses from your family line off of your life and declare them to be null and void. (Be as specific as possible.)
Acts of Sin	♦ By the blood of Jesus, I declare that all of your sins are forgiven and I forbid all the charges of sin against you from having any impact on your life. ♦ In the name of Jesus, I command the voice of the accuser to be silent including all guilt, shame, and fear of punishment associated with your sins, past, present, and future.
Curse of the Law	♦ In the name of Jesus, I declare the curse of the Law is broken off of your life. ♦ In the power and authority of the name of Jesus, I forbid all affliction, oppression, torment, and belittlement from having any right to restrict the blessings that God has for you.
Kingdom of Darkness	♦ In the power and authority of the name of Jesus, I command Satan to get behind you. ♦ In the power and authority of the name of Jesus, I break off all attachment to false spirituality and religion in your life, including any fortunes told about my life, spells cast, or curses spoken against you. ♦ By the blood of Jesus, I release you from all unwise vows that I/you have made and I reckon their entanglements null and void. ♦ In the power and authority of the name of Jesus, I command all voices of divination and false prophecy to be silent.
Personal Attributes	♦ By the blood of Jesus, I forbid the record of your past and your performance from having any effect on your life. ♦ In the power and authority of the name of Jesus, I command your flesh to be dead to the world and the pride of life.

We have been crucified, forgiven, redeemed, transferred, and delivered by the blood of Jesus.

---

5 – Death to Life – Actsheet #5
RAISED WITH CHRIST

Transformed	Free to do the Father's Will
New Creation	♦ By the blood of Jesus, I command your conscience to be cleansed from all consciousness of sin. I command your mind and every thought into captivity to *the obedience of Christ*. ♦ You are not the product of your past or your performance but of Christ's perfect work of obedience. ♦ Because of the blood of Jesus, ***you have no history of sin***, and God does not remember your sins against you. ♦ In Christ's righteousness, you stand before God as one who is holy, spotless, blameless, unreproveable, as if you had never sinned. ♦ By faith you are now in the bloodline of Jesus Christ. ♦ In Christ, you are a child of God.
Child of God	♦ Father, in the name of Jesus, I ask you to lead [their name] by your Holy Spirit. ♦ Father, I ask you to give [their name] wisdom from above. ♦ Father, show [their name] who he/she is in Christ and what you want him/her to do.

We have been reconciled, sanctified, made holy, and blessed with every spiritual blessing in Christ.

❧Additional Death to Life Activation

Water Baptism

Baptism is an outward demonstration of the change that took place in our heart when we believed Jesus Christ as our Lord and Savior. Christ commanded all of His disciples to baptize new disciples in the name of the Father, the Son, and the Holy Spirit. (Matthew 28:19) Baptism in Christ's day was done through full immersion under water. In fact, even Jesus was baptized in this way. For believers today, this kind of baptism symbolizes our inclusion in Christ's death and resurrection. Our old self dies as it is submerged under the water and we emerge out of the water as a new creation in Christ. If you or anyone in your group has not been water baptized, it can be done by your fellow disciples in any body of water, including a bathtub. Here's how:

Before baptizing someone, affirm their faith. ▪ Ask them: *"Do you believe that Jesus is Lord?"* and *"Do you believe that God raised Jesus from the dead?"* (see Romans 10:9-10) ▪ Wait for them to respond in sincere agreement.

Pray for them and listen to anything the Holy Spirit may desire for you to say to them at this very special time.

When you are both ready, say to them: "I baptize you in the name of the Father, the Son, and the Holy Spirit." ▪ Submerge them under the water and raise them up out of the water.

Rejoice! Affirm them as a child of God and as a new creation in Christ and welcome them into God's family.

Foot Washing

Jesus washed the feet of His disciples and said that we should do the same for one another. Once our whole body has been water baptized, foot washing is another outward demonstration of cleansing away the filth of sin and this world from our lives. (John 13:10)

Read John 13:3-16 and follow Jesus' example. ▪ Using a bucket of water, a chair, and a towel, take turns washing one another's feet.

❧

ACTIVITY 6
Pentecost

Every follower of Jesus is indwelt with the Holy Spirit and may have the Holy Spirit come upon them to supply power from heaven. In this Activity, we are going to pursue a Pentecost experience by inviting the Holy Spirit to come upon us and to speak to us. Then, we will listen for what God is speaking to us right now so that we align ourselves with His perfect and pleasing will.

This Activity will help you to:

- Pray for God's perfect will to be done
- Hear the promptings of the Holy Spirit for life today
- Become more confident in sharing what God is revealing to you

Introduction: Pentecost Experience[7]

Before the day of Pentecost, Jesus taught His disciples to pray, "Your Kingdom come, your will be done on earth as it is in heaven." Then on the day of Pentecost, the Holy Spirit came upon the disciples and they began to speak in tongues, uttering deep mysteries of God and praying for God's perfect will to be done in languages that were foreign to them.

As we seek to replicate a Pentecost experience, we will pray the same way that the disciples did and then listen for what the Holy Spirit is speaking to and through us. God often speaks to us in the form of a simple phrase, a picture that we see with the eyes of our heart, a sense that we know something that we have no other way of knowing, or an impression that comes to mind. What God reveals to us may be relevant to any individual within the group (even if we do not know who they may be) or may address the group as a whole. Some common ways that God speaks include but are not limited to:

- Declarations of the Gospel or of God's mercy and goodness
- Scripture verses or passages
- Words of encouragement, exhortation, and comfort
- Simple phrases or words (i.e. "mother-in-law" or "foot pain" or "freedom")
- Pictures or visions we see with the eyes of our heart (which we must then describe)
- Summonses to deeper trust in God and His ways
- Calls to repentance or rebuke for ungodliness or unbelief

This way of praying shifts our focus from our own will to being led by the Holy Spirit so that we can do

---

[7] For an in-depth teaching on the Holy Spirit dwelling within and coming upon believers, see *ACTS, Chapter 2: Holy Spirit* and *Chapter 6: Pentecost*

God's will.

Step One: Prepare

Distribute several index cards to everyone in the group or set up stacks of index cards that are easily accessible and within everyone's reach. ▪ Do not write anything on the index cards yet.

Allow a moment of stillness and silence.

♦ Invite the Holy Spirit to come upon you like He did on the day of Pentecost.

Step Two: Pray

Pray out loud for 5 minutes using one or more of the prayer methods below. Since everyone is praying out loud at the same time, speak in a tone of voice that is halfway between a whisper and your ordinary speaking volume. ▪ Repeat these phrases, blend them together, or speak fluently in tongues:

- ♦ Pray, "Come, Holy Spirit."
- ♦ Pray, "Your Kingdom come, Your will be done on earth as it is in heaven," (or pray the entire Lord's prayer)
- ♦ If you speak in tongues, pray in tongues.
- ♦ If you desire to speak in tongues but have never done so, ask God to help you to speak in tongues or use the other prayer methods above for now.[8]

While you pray, believe in your heart that you are praying perfect prayers to God. ▪ Resist and press through any feelings of discomfort, embarrassment, laughter, and awkwardness. ▪ Do your best to keep your thoughts focused on your prayers. ▪ Continue praying in this way for 5 whole minutes.

Step Three: Listen & Write

After 5 minutes of prayer has elapsed, stop speaking out loud and allow a moment of silence.

Open your spiritual ears to listen for what the Holy Spirit is saying. ▪ If there was *one thing* that you believe that God is saying right now to someone in your group (even if you do not know who it is) or to your group as a whole, what would it be? ▪ Remember, this could be a simple phrase, a picture you see with the eyes of your heart, or an impression that comes to mind, etc.

Write down on an index card *one thing* that you believe that the Holy Spirit is saying. ▪ Write one impression, insight, or revelation per index card. Use as many index cards as you need to.

Hand the index cards to the designated leader or spokesperson. ▪ Wait until several cards have been collected or until everyone is finished writing. This way, no one will know which person wrote which card and there is no need for embarrassment if anyone did not hear God correctly.

Step Four: Report & Receive

Have the leader or spokesperson slowly read the insights on the index cards out loud, one card at a time. ▪ Listen closely as each index card is read out loud.

---

[8] See Additional Activities at the end of this chapter.

Allow the Holy Spirit to prompt you when an insight given by someone else was God speaking to you or about your current situation. As a guideline,

- ◊ An insight for you will seem to catch your attention, resonate within you, or have a "stickiness" to it.
- ◊ If you are unsure as to whether something is for you or not, ask God for wisdom and wait for Him to reveal it to you in the course of time.
- ◊ If nothing seems to be God speaking to you today, then support those who did hear from God by praying for them.

Step Five: Pray

Divide into groups of three or four. • If you are comfortable doing so, share with your small group an insight that you believe God was speaking to you. • Allow each person the opportunity to share how God spoke to them.

After everyone in the small group has shared which insight resonated with them, pray for one another based on this new insight from God. For example:

- ◊ Thank God for speaking this word to them.
- ◊ Ask God for wisdom about what was revealed.
- ◊ Listen for anything else the Holy Spirit may be revealing to them or about this issue.
- ◊ Pray as you normally would for them based on this new insight from God.

Onward to Maturity:

This method of prayer can be used for extended prayer times and without index cards. Advance from 5 minutes to 20 minutes, to one hour or more. Progress from submitting index cards after prayer to submitting them and reading them out loud as you go and praying together about the insights God supplies. Eventually, put the index cards away and use this as your primary approach to prayer. Listen to God as you pray, share your insights out loud as you hear them from the Holy Spirit, and pray together about what God reveals to you, one insight at a time. Return to this exercise whenever you want to pray God's perfect will or when you do not know how to pray.

The aim of this activity is to be filled with the Holy Spirit and to pray the perfect will of God.

♨Additional Pentecost Activation

Filling with Holy Spirit

In addition to outpourings of the Holy Spirit such as the believers experienced on the day of Pentecost, disciples were also filled with the Holy Spirit through the laying on of hands. If you or anyone in your group has not experienced being filled with the Holy Spirit or desires a fresh infilling, other believers can lay hands on them.

Surround the person receiving the Holy Spirit and place one or both hands on them in an appropriate place. • Believe in your heart that God is filling the recipient with the Holy Spirit through your hands as you pray. Think of it like filling a spiritual gas tank and the gas is flowing into their spiritual tank through your hands.

Pray something like this out loud as the Holy Spirit leads you:

- ♨ "Father, in the name of Jesus, please fill [their name] with Your Holy Spirit."
- ♨ "Father, in the name of Jesus, fill [their name] to the full with your Holy Spirit."
- ♨ "Father, give [their name] more of You and more of Your Holy Spirit."
- ♨ "Come, Holy Spirit."

Allow for a moment of silence as God works. • Release your hands. • Ask the recipient to say *one thing* that they believe that the Holy Spirit is saying. The word that they speak may or may not be spoken in tongues.

On an ongoing basis, you can pray for yourself for a fresh infilling of the Holy Spirit even if other believers are not present to lay hands on you.

Tongues and Interpretation in a Group Setting

Whenever believers are gathered together, God may speak through a person in a language that is foreign to them. In a group setting, words from the Lord that are given in tongues must be interpreted. The Holy Spirit can enable any believer to bring a word in tongues and/or interpret words that are given in tongues. Sometimes when we pray in tongues, we pray real languages that are foreign to us but that someone else speaks fluently and can interpret for us what God is saying. Other times, we are speaking the languages of angels and the Holy Spirit must supply the interpretation into our own language.

If you have a word from the Lord in tongues, wait for an appropriate time to speak. • Then, say the word in tongues out loud for everyone to hear. • If you have the interpretation of what God was saying through the word in tongues, then share the interpretation. • If you do not know what God was saying through your word in tongues, be still and silent and wait for someone else to interpret the word. • Do not move forward with the meeting until the word in tongues has been interpreted. • Seek the Lord in prayer together until someone has an interpretation of what God is saying. Use Step Two and Step Three of this Activity as a guide.

ACTIVITY 7
Cast Out Demons

Jesus cast demons out of people in order to set them free from torments, afflictions, and sicknesses and this was done as a clear demonstration of His supreme power and authority over the evil one and the powers of darkness. Then, Jesus shared His anointing for setting captives free and sent His disciples to cast out demons in His name, power, and authority.[9] In this Activity, we will identify and cast out demons (also referred to as unclean spirits) so that we are set free from things which have afflicted and tormented us and can be truly filled to full measure with the Holy Spirit.

This Activity will help you to:

⚶ Function in your authority in Christ

⚶ Experience the power of the Gospel of Jesus Christ

⚶ Discern spirits and problems which may be the result of unclean spirits

⚶ Be set free and give the gift of freedom to others

⚶ Be filled afresh with the Holy Spirit

Introduction and Precautions: Casting Out Demons – Please Read

!! Note: Please have everyone in your group read this section so that they are forewarned and strengthened to maintain their freedom in Christ.

Christ followers cannot be possessed by demons, but we can be oppressed and otherwise harassed by unclean spirits. This can be the cause of compulsions, addictions, and chronic behaviors which plague us with trouble. However, when we function in the power and authority of the name of Jesus, the demons must leave us and cease torturing us. Deliverance to freedom from things that have oppressed us for years can happen in an instant.

This said, we are responsible for maintaining our freedom by repenting from old ways of thinking and doing things and by placing our faith fully in Christ alone. Oftentimes, the unclean spirits have caused certain behavioral patterns in our lives over the course of many years which must be altered or renounced altogether. Once the unclean spirits have been expelled, our behavior must also be modified in order to not allow the expelled demons to return to us. This can be more challenging because, even though we dislike the lows created by the unclean spirits, there are often highs that we experience from the behavior that we enjoy. For example, a person oppressed by a spirit of alcoholism may be in the habit of visiting the local pub every night at six o'clock. If the alcoholic spirit is expelled from them on a Monday night but they return to the pub on Tuesday night, it is no longer the demon compelling them to

---

[9] For an in-depth study on our power and authority in Christ, see *ACTS, Chapter 7: Kingdom*

do so but their own behavioral habit.

Therefore, when we receive freedom from demonic oppression we must also commit ourselves to being led by the Holy Spirit into paths of righteousness and not continuing in our old ways and habits. Through Christ, God gives us power to change. This is significant because Jesus warned that once an unclean spirit leaves a person, it goes off and then returns with seven other spirits that are more evil than it is in order to attempt re-entry. If the demons are able to penetrate successfully, then the person is worse off than they were before they were set free in the first place. (see Luke 11:24-26) The only way to not give place to the returning spirits is to be full of another spirit—the Holy Spirit.

Therefore, as you engage in this Activity, receive your freedom from unclean spirits as a free gift from God through faith in Jesus Christ and due to the power and authority that we have in His name. But, be certain that you are ready to change and are ready to be finished with everything in your life that is related to whatever unclean spirits you have expelled from you. Be filled with the Holy Spirit so that you remain free in Christ and are empowered to do the will of God for your life.

Step One: Identify Demonic Oppression

Demons or unclean spirits can be the cause of compulsions, addictions, and irrational behaviors that have a tendency to spiral out of control. They may entice you beyond your ability to resist or cause you to make a moral exception to the rule in certain areas of life even if you are otherwise a highly virtuous person. Sometimes when an unclean spirit is functioning in or through you, it does not even seem like you because it is so unlike you to behave this way and yet, you are. Other times, it causes you to do something that you truly do not want to do but, no matter how much you resist or try to exert self-control, you are overwhelmed or overpowered and you do it anyway. Demons may cause you emotional torment, shame, or compel self-mutilation, self-loathing, or violence against yourself. Most times, demons will not cause you to be violent towards others but rather toward yourself. This is not to say that others are unaffected by your behavior, but typically other people are not the target of your oppression…you are. Their aim is to block your faith in Christ, stunt your ability to fulfill God's purposes for your life, and ultimately to destroy you.

Some common demons and unclean spirits include but are not limited to:

Anger	Sexual spirits	Rejection	Infirmity
Fear	Self-loathing	Religion	New Age spirits
Anxiety	Abandonment	Hopelessness	Bitterness
Depression	Jezebel	Witchcraft	Divination
Regret	Offense	Manipulation	Leviathan

If you are suffering from unexplainable oppression in your life, it may be due to unclean spirits such as these. In addition to these, there are countless other unclean spirits that can cause us unnecessary torment and which we can overcome by the power of God through Christ.

Step Two: Discern Spirits for Yourself

⟡ Ask the Holy Spirit to give you the gift of discerning of spirits.

Ask the Holy Spirit to reveal to you any demonic or unclean spirits which have been afflicting or oppressing you. • Write down what you hear the Holy Spirit saying to you. • If you cannot summarize it in one word, write a brief description articulating what the unclean spirit causes. For example, "A spirit that causes you to always feel like you are on the outside looking in."

Step Three: Repent and Prepare

Look over the list of unclean spirits that the Holy Spirit has identified for you.

Allow for several moments of stillness and silence. • Talk to God about how this unclean spirit has affected your life and the lives of your loved ones. • Receive God's forgiveness as a free gift through the blood of Jesus.

Decide in your heart that you are ready to change. • If you are not ready to repent in this area of your life or renounce the behaviors associated with it, then do not proceed to the next step. • Allow the Holy Spirit to speak to you and to minister to you until you are ready to change.

Step Four: Believe in the Power of the Gospel

If you are ready to be set free from demonic oppression, then the first thing you have to do is believe:

⟡ Believe in your heart that Jesus conquered all darkness, evil, and death so that you could be free.
⟡ Believe in your heart that because of the blood of Jesus, unclean spirits have no right to afflict you or have any dominion in you.
⟡ Believe in your heart that as a disciple of Christ, all power and authority has been given to you in His name to command and cast out demons and unclean spirits the same way that Jesus did.

Step Five: Command and Expel[10]

In your inmost being, take your position of authority in Christ. • Imagine yourself commanding a well-trained dog, knowing that it must obey you. This said, even a well-trained dog knows when you are serious and really mean your commands, so make sure that you utter your commands with confidence and authority in Jesus' name.

Keep your eyes open. • While believing in your heart that the demons are leaving, command the unclean spirits to leave you. • Use the following commands as a guide:

⟡ In the power and authority of the name of Jesus, I command spirits of [name of unclean spirit] to leave right now and never return.
⟡ I am protected by the blood of the Lamb, Jesus Christ, and in Jesus' name I command [name of unclean spirit] to leave right now.
⟡ In the power and authority of the name of Jesus, I drive out [name of unclean spirit] from its root.

---

[10] Anyone who does not believe that Jesus is Lord and that God raised Him from the dead should abstain from commanding demons in Jesus' name. (see Acts 19:11-16)

- In the name of Jesus Christ, I command [name of unclean spirit] and all of its associates or comrades to leave and go to the place that the Lord Jesus sends you.
- If you do not have a specific name for a spirit: In the power and authority of the name of Jesus, I command unclean spirits to leave right now and never return.
- If you are uncertain whether it is demonic or not: In the power and authority of the name of Jesus, I command all dark places to be made light right now.

After commanding the unclean spirits to leave, take a deep breath in and exhale forcefully. • Repeat this a few times. • Note: The word for spirit in both Hebrew and Greek is the same word that is used for breath. Oftentimes, by breathing out deeply, we give the unclean spirits a way to exit.

Repeat the commands and deep exhaling two to three times or until you feel settled in your heart that it is finished.

Note: Sometimes demons and unclean spirits cause physical manifestations which can be unsettling if you do not recognize what is happening. If you experience anything unusual while you are commanding demons to leave you or even in the days following the expulsion of demons, do not be afraid. Repeat the commands above and maintain faith in your heart that all demons and unclean spirits must bow to and obey your command in the name of Jesus.

Believe in your heart that the unclean spirits have left you or are on their way out due to your command. • Praise God for His deliverance and the freedom that He has given you in Christ.

Step Six: Cast Demons Out of One Another

Depending on the size of your group, partner up two-by-two or gather into small groups of three or four.

Select one person to receive ministry. They are the Recipient. • The other partner or members of the small group are the Ministers.

Repeat Steps Two through Five of this Activity, except discern and command unclean spirits to leave the Recipient. • Read through the following instructions before you begin.

Recipient: Allow the Holy Spirit to reveal to those who are ministering to you the unclean spirits that may be impacting your life. Agree, disagree, or clarify as needed but try to keep it brief in order to stay focused on receiving freedom. • While you are receiving ministry, exhale deeply and believe in your heart that the demons are leaving at the command of those ministering to you.

Ministers: Ask the Holy Spirit to help you to discern any demons or unclean spirits that are affecting the Recipient. • Share with the Recipient what the Holy Spirit reveals to you. • Ask them if they are ready to be set free by the power of God in the name of Jesus. • Believe in your heart that, in the name of Jesus, the demons and unclean spirits in them must obey your command to leave. • Keep your eyes open and look at the Recipient but speak to the spirits within them. • Command the spirits afflicting the Recipient to leave using the commands given in Step Five as a guide.

Change Recipients and repeat until everyone who desires to receive ministry has been ministered to.

Step Seven: Refill – Important

✷ Ask the Holy Spirit to fill you to full measure with Christ.

Allow for a moment of stillness and silence. ▪ Receive the Spirit of the Lord in your inmost being. ▪ Imagine that every place in your soul that was occupied by the unclean spirits is now occupied with the Holy Spirit.

Step Eight: Praise God and Testify

Praise God in your heart for what He has done for you.

Invite anyone in your group who is comfortable doing so to share with the group what the Lord just set them free from or any immediate results of freedom that they received or experienced.

Onward to Maturity:

Jesus was filled to full measure with the Holy Spirit. He discerned and commanded demonic and unclean spirits to leave the people that they were oppressing as a part of His daily life as the Son of God. As children of God through faith in Christ, we can be free of all oppression, be filled with the Holy Spirit, and set captives free wherever we go. Return to this Activity any time you sense that an oppression or compulsion in your own life or the life of another person is the result of demons or unclean spirits.

The aim of this activity is be totally free from demonic oppression
and to function fully in our authority in Christ against the forces of evil.

⸙Additional Cast Out Demons Activation

Spiritual House Cleaning

Sometimes spaces or places can contain unclean or demonic spirits. This can be due to things that took place in their history, due to ungodly activities conducted by past or present owners, or due to demonic attack against its inhabitants. When forces of evil are at work in a place, it may seem heavy, dark, uneasy, charged with strange energy, or devoid of life. Sometimes, strange or bizarre occurrences may happen in these places with a level of frequency which rules out coincidence. This said, when a follower of Christ is the owner, possessor, or resident of a place or space, we have authority in the name of Jesus to command all evil, darkness, demons, and unclean spirits to leave. Here's how:

Go to the place or space which may be affected by forces of darkness. • Bring anointing oil with you as a symbol of the Holy Spirit. • No matter what happens, do not be afraid. Forces of darkness feed on fear but in Christ, we have nothing to be afraid of. • Believe in your heart that unclean spirits must leave at your command in the power and authority of the name of Jesus.

Remove everything that has any connection to all forms of spirituality that are not rooted in Christ, including idols, books, propaganda, tools, special clothes, etc. For example: Astrology books, Ouija boards, tarot cards, dream catchers, unclean music, Buddha's, magic wands, spiritual incense burners, books of spells or sorcery, cloaks, jewels, or accessories used in non-Christian worship, or anything that has been used in the process of accessing the spiritual realm. • Throw all of these items away and take them off of the premises or burn them.

Before you begin walking around the space, open a few windows to give unclean spirits a way to exit, or leave the door slightly ajar if it is safe to do so.

⸙ Ask the Holy Spirit to give you the gift of discerning of spirits.

Walk around the place and ask the Holy Spirit to reveal to you any demonic or unclean spirits which have taken up residence there. • Remain attentive to what the Holy Spirit reveals to you.

Use the anointing oil to make the sign of the cross on the doors and windows or points of entry and exit. Remember how the Hebrews painted the blood of the Passover Lamb on their doorposts so that the destroyer could not enter. (see Exodus 12) • As you anoint the doors and windows, say something like, "In the name of Jesus, no evil is permitted in this place."

When you hear the Holy Spirit reveal an unclean spirit to you in a certain area, stop walking. • Stretch out your hand towards the area and command the unclean spirit to leave. Here are the sample commands as an example:

- ⸙ In the power and authority of the name of Jesus, I command spirits of [name of unclean spirit] to leave right now and never return.
- ⸙ This place is protected by the blood of the Lamb, Jesus Christ, and in Jesus' name I command [name of unclean spirit] to leave.
- ⸙ In the power and authority of the name of Jesus, I drive out [name of unclean spirit] from its root.

- ⟐ In the name of Jesus Christ, I command [name of unclean spirit] and all of its associates or comrades to leave and go to the place that the Lord Jesus sends you.
- ⟐ If you do not have a specific name for a spirit but you sense that something is off in the space: In the power and authority of the name of Jesus, I command unclean spirits to leave right now and never return.
- ⟐ If you sense that something is wrong but are uncertain whether it is demonic or not: In the power and authority of the name of Jesus, I command all dark places to be made light right now.

Once you have finished commanding unclean spirits and forces of darkness to leave, speak a blessing in the same place in the name of Jesus. For example, say things such as:

- ⟐ May the peace of God rest upon this place, in Jesus' name.
- ⟐ Let there be light in this place, in Jesus' name.
- ⟐ Lord Jesus, bestow your blessing upon this place.
- ⟐ May God's Kingdom come into this place and make it on earth as it is in heaven.

Praise God for cleaning the space or place for you.

ACTIVITY 8
Prophesy

Every believer in Jesus Christ has the ability to prophesy. When we prophesy to one another, we do so to strengthen, encourage, and comfort one another in God's love for us and His plans for us. In this Activity, we will prophesy to one another, meaning that we will listen to the Lord for one another and share with one another what we believe God is saying.

This Activity will help you to:

- Listen for and discern what the Holy Spirit may be saying to someone else
- Become more confident in sharing what God is revealing to you
- Discern when the Lord is speaking to you through someone else
- Deepen your understanding of God's love for you and His purposes
- Become more confident in doing God's will for your life

Introduction: Prophesy

To prophesy simply means to speak by divine inspiration as God's representative. As followers of Christ, we are enabled by the Holy Spirit to speak the words of God. This could be in the form of a simple phrase, a picture that we see with the eyes of our heart, a sense that we know something that we have no other way of knowing, or an impression that comes to mind about, or for, the recipients of our prophesying. Some common ways that God speaks prophetically through us include but are not limited to:

- Scripture verses or passages relevant to their life right now
- Simple phrases which hold significance to them even if we do not understand what it means
- Pictures or visions we see with the eyes of our heart (which we must then describe to them)
- Revelation of their Kingdom purpose or call of God on their life
- Discernment of the time or season of life with God that they are in and God's purpose in it
- Insight into an area of their life which God desires to heal through His love
- Summonses to deeper trust in God and His ways
- Warnings of danger ahead
- Calls to repentance or rebuke for ungodliness or unbelief

As we prophesy, we cooperate with God in order to accurately communicate what He is saying to the recipient. We must be careful not to add to God's words through presumption or leave anything out because it is unclear to us. What may not seem to make sense to us may be the very word that the recipient understands and needs to hear.

When we receive prophetic words from others, we listen with our spirit in order to discern the words of God. As a general guideline, the Holy Spirit speaks truth, encourages faith, testifies to eternal hope, imparts God's unconditional love, and conveys God's work on our behalf for our good. On the other hand, words of guilt, shame, fear, punishment, accusation, curse, or manipulation to have personal desires fulfilled are not from the Holy Spirit. We can receive words from the Holy Spirit as the words of God Himself to us and we should reject words that are not from the Holy Spirit, rendering them powerless in our lives by the blood of Jesus. This said, just because we reject a prophetic word in whole or in part, or a prophetic word that we deliver is rejected by the recipient, does not mean that the Holy Spirit was not speaking to us or through us. Listen carefully and remember that even Jesus' prophetic words were rejected by people who should have received them.

Prophesying is best when we keep it simple: Listen to God and do your best to say or communicate what He says or reveals to you.

Step One: Prepare

Gather into small groups of equal size, ideally three to four people per group. ▪ It is preferable to do this with people that you do not know well so move around if you need to.

Distribute index cards so that each person has enough index cards to prophesy to each person in the group. ▪ Do not write anything on the index cards yet.

Decide amongst your small group who will be the first person to receive prophetic words. ▪ They are the Recipient.

Step Two: Listen to God

🔥 Allow a moment of stillness and silence. Invite the Holy Spirit to come and speak to you.

Focus your attention on the Recipient. ▪ Write their first name on one of the index cards. ▪ If you are the Recipient, be still and silent for now.

Allow a moment or two of silence in the presence of God as you listen to God for the Recipient. ▪ Listen carefully to what the Holy Spirit reveals to you as you focus your attention on the Recipient. ▪ Remember, it could be a simple phrase, a picture you see with the eyes of your heart, a sense that you know something that you have no other way of knowing, an impression that comes to mind, etc. ▪ Resist presuming what you think God would say to the Recipient. ▪ Also, when you hear the Holy Spirit speak, resist analyzing, intellectualizing, or trying to figure out what God means or what you think the Recipient needs to do. (This can be more challenging if you know the Recipient well.)

Step Three: Write Insights

On the index card with the Recipient's name on it, write down *one thing* that you believe God is saying to them right now. ▪ If it seems unclear to you, do your best to write down your impression of what the Holy Spirit has revealed to you.

Hand all of the cards to the Recipient at the same time. This way, the Recipient will not know which person gave which word and there is no need for embarrassment if you did not hear God correctly. • If you are the Recipient, put your index cards off to the side for now.

Step Four: Repeat for Others

Decide amongst your group who will be the next to receive prophetic words. • They are now the Recipient.

Repeat Step Two and Step Three for that person.

Repeat again until each person has received prophetic words.

Step Five: Discern and Receive or Reject

After everyone has received prophetic words from their groups, each person should have a small stack of index cards with their name and prophetic insights on them.

Silently and slowly read the insights on each index card that you received. • Pay attention to whether the Holy Spirit is directing you in agreement or rejection of what is written on each card. As a guideline:

- If the Holy Spirit agrees with what is written, consider the prophetic word to be from God and receive it.
- If the Holy Spirit is not in agreement with what is written or it seems to be accusatory or condemning, reject the word as error and do not permit it to penetrate your thoughts.
- If you are uncertain in any way whether the prophetic word is from God or not, do not receive or reject it. Ask God for wisdom and wait for Him to reveal it to you in the course of time.

Take several moments of silence to ponder the prophetic words that you have received from God. • Allow the words that you have received to penetrate deeply into your heart.

Step Six: Pray

Share with your small group one insight that you received that you believe is God speaking to you today. • After everyone in the small group has shared one insight that resonated with them, pray for them based on this prophetic insight from God. For example:

- Thank God for speaking this word to them
- Ask God for more wisdom about what was revealed
- Listen for additional prophetic insights from the Holy Spirit and share it with them
- Pray as you normally would for them based on this insight from God

Onward to Maturity: Prophesy 24/7

Once you are confident in your ability to hear God and prophesy to others, do this Activity without index cards. Practice prophesying by listening for prophetic words as you engage with other people through the course of your normal day and speak them to people as the Holy Spirit enables you. God may want to speak through you at any time to family, friends, strangers, or groups of people. Oftentimes, more extended prophesying is simply piecing together one divine insight after another through listening to

God and relaying to the recipient what we hear from the Holy Spirit as we go. Stay engaged with the Holy Spirit as you prophesy so that you do not add or leave out anything of significance. As God's representative, be diligent to convey His message as best you are able.

The aim of this activity is to speak the words of God to others.

♦Additional Prophesy Activation

Prophesying About Situations, Cities, Nations

Listening to God for prophetic insights into situations, cities, and nations can be done in the same way that we listen to God for individuals. The situation, city, or nation becomes the Recipient of your prophetic words.

Start by using the index card method, following Step Two and Step Three of this Activity. • Delegate someone in the group to read out loud the prophetic insights that you have received from God.

Use Step Five as a guideline for listening to the Holy Spirit's agreement or disagreement about the prophetic words as they are being read out loud. • Discuss amongst yourselves the prophetic insights that you believe to be from God for that situation, city, or nation.

Use Step Six as a guide and pray for the situation, city, or nation based on the insights that God has given you.

Prophesying in Group Settings

Whenever believers are gathered together, God may desire to speak a prophetic word to or for the benefit of the whole group of people. Any believer is able to bring a word from the Lord to share with the whole group and others who are present discern whether they believe the word to be from God or not.

♦If you are unsure whether or not it is appropriate to prophesy:

Write your insights on an index card and give the card to the leader or person in authority over the group or meeting. This honors the leader who is responsible for discerning whether or not the prophetic word is fitting for the group or meeting. • The leader may share your insights with the whole group or invite you to do so. • If the leader does not authorize you to share the prophetic word, then submit to their authority and cooperate with the purpose of the meeting.

♦If prophetic words are welcomed:

Wait for an appropriate time to speak so that only one person is prophesying at a time. • Share what you sense that God is saying with the group. • Others listen and discern if God is speaking.

♦If your word is in contrast to the tone or topic that is already in prayer or discussion:

Allow everyone to finish praying about the subject already at hand and then share your insight. • Alternatively, while everyone continues praying, privately share your insight with the leader or person in authority, giving the leader the opportunity to agree or disagree with the change of subject. The leader may share your insights with the whole group or invite you to do so. • If the leader does not authorize or overrules the change of topic or tone, then submit to their authority and cooperate with the purpose of the meeting.

♦

♦

ACTIVITY 9
Love One Another

Jesus gave one new command to His disciples, *"Love one another as I have loved you."* This kind of love is only possible when the Holy Spirit and nature of Christ is working in us and through us. In this Activity, we will use the passages of 1 Corinthians 13:4-8 and 1 John 4:7-8 to recognize and receive the ways that God loves us so that we can love one another the way that He loves us.

This Activity will help you to:

* Gain a deeper understanding of the practical ways that God loves you
* Increase your ability to receive God's love
* Identify ways that you can be more loving towards others
* Let go of past hurts and disappointments
* Grow in the love of God

Step One: God's Love

Prepare: Find the Love One Another Actsheet. (See also: www.activatedchurch.com/actsheets) • Designate one person to be the Reader or decide to rotate around the group with each person reading one phrase at a time.

* Allow for a moment of stillness and silence. • Focus your attention on the place in your heart that loves Jesus. (This is the Holy Spirit of Christ in you.)

Reader(s): Read the *God's Love for Me in Christ* phrases found on the top half of the page out loud at a slow pace. • As the phrases are read out loud, open your heart as an object of God's love.

Allow several moments of silence in the presence of God. • Allow God's love for you to commune with the place in your heart that loves Jesus. • If you become distracted, use the following as a guideline:

* If you become sidetracked by other thoughts, refocus your attention on the part of your heart that loves Jesus.
* If you feel unworthy of God's love or find it difficult to receive, focus your attention on Jesus who died for you so that God's love for you is a free gift, even though none of us deserve it.

Talk to God briefly about any resistances you encounter in receiving His love. • Invite the Holy Spirit to minister to you in these areas. • Make a concerted effort to release the areas of resistance and allow God's love to penetrate deeply into your heart.

Step Two: Love for Others

Reader(s): Read the *God's Love through Me to Others* phrases found on the bottom half of the page out loud at a slow pace. ▪ As the phrases are read out loud, open your heart as a vessel of God's love to others.

Allow several moments of silence in the presence of God. ▪ Use the eyes of your heart to picture God's love flowing through you to others. ▪ If you become obstructed or frustrated, use the following as a guideline:

- ◊ If you become focused on past experiences that may have caused you to become guarded, defensive, or unloving, remember that God does not hold your offenses against you. Jesus took the punishment that you deserve. Ask Him to teach you to love like that.
- ◊ If you encounter areas of unforgiveness or bitterness towards others, focus on Jesus who was crucified by the ones He came to save and forgave them while He was still on the cross. Ask Him to teach you to love like that.
- ◊ If you seem to be blocked from loving others in a godly way, ask God to reveal what the reason is and allow the Holy Spirit to minister to you in these areas.

Talk to God briefly about any reasons why you find it difficult to love the way that He does. ▪ Invite the Holy Spirit to minister to you in these areas so that you receive healing for your wounds, mercy for your unforgiveness, and freedom in blocked areas. ▪ Make a concerted effort to open your heart to love again.

Step Three: Pray for One Another & Take Action

Partner up with one other person. ▪ Share with one another one aspect of receiving God's love and one aspect of extending love to others that stood out to you. ▪ If you are comfortable doing so, share an area of difficulty that you have experienced in receiving or extending love, and/or any emotional wounds that need God's healing.

Pray for one another to grow deeper in God's love. ▪ Ask for God to heal emotional wounds from past experiences and to fill you with fresh hope. ▪ Ask God to give you opportunities this week to receive more of His love and to be more loving towards others.

As you go through your week, ask the Holy Spirit to help you to take every opportunity to love others the way that He loves you.

Onward to Maturity: Love 24/7

God is love and the more that we genuinely and unconditionally love others, the more we are like Him. As we grow towards Christlikeness, we become more like Jesus who revealed God's love by laying down His life for us and giving to us what we do not deserve. Return to this Activity anytime you find it difficult to receive God's love or to love others the way that He loves you.

The aim of this activity is to love the way that God loves.

9 – Love One Another - Actsheet
GOD'S LOVE FOR ME AND THROUGH ME

──────────────── GOD'S LOVE FOR ME IN CHRIST ────────────────

God is always patient with me. God is always kind to me.

God does not envy me and He is not jealous of me.

God does not boast that He is better than I am. God is not arrogant or rude towards me.

God does not insist on His own way and He has given me free will.

God is not irritable or resentful towards me even when I make mistakes or fail.

God does not rejoice at wrongdoing in any situation by me or by others.

God rejoices when the truth is revealed and when the right thing is done in all situations.

God bears all things with me and for me and sent Jesus to take the punishment that I deserve.

God believes the best in me and has confidence in who He made me to be.

God hopes and confidently expects the best for me.

God endures all things with me. He does not abandon me and He is always with me.

God's love towards me never fades or weakens because of my circumstances or failures.

God's love never fails me.

──────────────── GOD'S LOVE THROUGH ME TO OTHERS ────────────────

I am patient, even when things take longer than I want them to.

I am kind, even when things do not go my way.

I am not jealous and I do not want what I do not have.

I do not boast in my own abilities. I am not proud and I do not consider myself superior.

I am not rude. I do not insist on my own way.

I am not irritable or resentful when things do not go the way that I want them to.

I do not enjoy, approve of, or celebrate wrongdoing in any situation.

I rejoice when the truth is revealed, and when God's will is done on earth as it is in heaven.

I bear all things even when I suffer for other people's mistakes.

I believe the best in others and have confidence in who God designed them to be.

I hope and expect the best for others, even if they do not deserve it.

I endure all things with others and I do not abandon them.

My love for others does not fade or weaken. My love never fails.

♦Additional Love One Another Activation

The earliest disciples of Christ devoted themselves to fellowship with one another. (see Acts 2:42) When we truly know that everything we possess is a free gift from God, we are free to share what we have with others because we consider nothing to be our own. (see Acts 4:32) Sharing our time, resources, and abilities for each other's benefit is one of the primary ways that we reveal God's love to the world. Here are some practical ways to devote yourselves to fellowship with one another.

Share a Meal Together

Select a time when your group meets to enjoy a meal together in the place of your regular prayer or Bible study. On that day, try to have each person bring one part of the meal. Have those who are able to bring more do so and let those who cannot bring anything come empty handed. ▪ Enjoy a relaxed time of conversation and getting to know one another better. ▪ Do this on a regular basis.

Collect an Offering

Collect an offering for someone in your group. Have everyone in the group contribute something to the offering, even if it is a promise or an *I owe you* to serve them in some way, such bring them a meal, clean their house, watch their children, or fix their bookshelf. ▪ Then, give it to the person privately or publicly, depending on their personality. ▪ Expect nothing in return from them and be sure to follow through on the commitments you make to serve them.

Reverse Offering

Using index cards without names on them, have each person write one thing that they are in need of and cannot acquire or accomplish for themselves at this time.

Hand the cards to the leader or designated spokesperson. Have the leader or spokesperson read the index cards out loud. ▪ As the cards are read out loud, listen for anything that you have and are willing to give or are able and willing to do. (If needed, leave a moment for spouses to discuss what they are able and willing to do.)

After all the cards have been read, say out loud anything that you heard that you are able and willing to share. ▪ Allow for the person in need to approach you during or after your meeting so that you can attend to their need.

Reach Out and Visit

Go to visit anyone in your group who is ill, injured, in the hospital, in prison, is grieving a loss, is particularly isolated, or who has not been to your group for a while. ▪ If you cannot visit them, call them or write them a note. ▪ Pray with them. ▪ Do this often, even if there is no obvious reason to do so. Love them the way that God loves you.

ACTIVITY 10
Heal the Sick

In His earthly ministry, Jesus healed all manner of sickness (see Matthew 4:23) and gave His disciples authority over every disease (see Matthew 10:1) so that they could heal the sick and even raise the dead in His name, power, and authority.[11] In this Activity, we will practice healing the sick the way that Jesus and His disciples did.

This Activity will help you to:

- ٨ Function in your power and authority in Christ
- ٨ Receive healing for your ailments and diseases
- ٨ Minister healing to the sick

Introduction: Healing in Christ[12]

On the cross, Jesus took upon Himself all of our sicknesses, diseases, and pains so that we can be healed, made whole, and function on earth as it is in heaven. Healing is not a matter of whether or not God will or will not heal. God already healed by the stripes of Jesus and through His death and resurrection. Jesus atoned for our sin, conquered the devil, and redeemed us from the curse which includes every kind of sickness, disease, and infirmity—even those not specifically mentioned by name. (see Deuteronomy 28:61) This means that sickness and disease have absolutely no place in us when we believe what Christ completed. Healing is as finished as our salvation in Christ and is available for us to receive as a free gift by grace through faith. With repentance, trust in Christ's finished work, and a mustard seed of faith, we can receive our healing from God with no harmful side-effects.

If you do not yet believe that healing is a finished work or are uncertain in any way, then tell God that you believe Jesus and ask Him to help your unbelief in the area of healing. Ask the Holy Spirit to give you revelation of our healing in Christ and study the Scriptures until you are fully persuaded that, by the stripes of Jesus, we were healed. (1 Peter 2:24)

Step One: Testify to Build Faith

Hearing the stories of how Jesus healed other people builds our faith to believe for receiving and ministering healing.

Ask if anyone in the group has a story of how God miraculously healed them (or someone they know) without the intervention of man or medicine. ▪ Invite a few of them to share the story of God's miraculous

---

[11] For an in-depth study on our power and authority in Christ, see *ACTS, Chapter 7: Kingdom*

[12] For a brief study on healing, see *ACTS, Chapter 10: Miracles*

healing.

Alternatively, research stories of how Jesus has healed people and read one or two of them out loud to the group. • If you do not have access to stories of more recent healings of Jesus, read a few healing stories from the Scriptures, particularly the Gospels. Here are a few passages that may encourage you and build your faith:

Matthew 8:1-4	Mark 3:1-6	Luke 7:11-17	John 11:38-44
Matthew 8:14-17	Mark 7:31-37	Luke 22:47-51	Acts 3:1-10
Matthew 9:1-8	Mark 10:46-52	John 5:1-9	Acts 9:32-35
Matthew 9:27-31	Luke 14:1-6	John 9:1-7	Isaiah 53:1-12

Step Two: Believe in Your Heart

⚘ Ask the Holy Spirit to fill you with God's power and to quicken your mortal body.

No matter what is ailing you, resist all forms of fear. • Keep your problem small in view of God's great power that raises the dead. No matter what is ailing you, your disease is smaller than death.

Receiving healing is an opportunity to engage your faith in Christ's finished work on your behalf. • Reaffirm your faith by believing these things in your heart:

- ⚘ Believe that healing in Christ is as easy to receive as salvation.
- ⚘ Believe that sickness is not God's will for you in Christ.
- ⚘ Believe that because of Jesus sickness has no right to you due to sin, the curse of the Law, or the devil.
- ⚘ Believe that all sicknesses, pains, and griefs were dealt with on the cross of Christ.
- ⚘ Believe that God's power through Christ is able to heal you.
- ⚘ Believe that it is God's will for you to be healed.
- ⚘ Believe that healing is available for you to receive as a free gift right now in Jesus' name.
- ⚘ Believe that by the stripes of Christ you were healed. (1 Peter 2:24) This verse is past tense. It is finished.

Step Three: Identify Sicknesses that God is Healing Today

Designate one person to be the Recorder. The Recorder is responsible for writing down the words of knowledge as the group speaks them out.

⚘ Ask the Holy Spirit to give you words of knowledge of specific ailments, infirmities, and diseases that God is healing today.

Allow a moment of stillness and silence. • Listen for words of knowledge from the Holy Spirit. • These could be as simple as "foot pain," "breast cancer," "depression," or "stiff neck." • Anyone in the group can receive a word of knowledge. • Note: Sometimes words of knowledge can be in the form of a sudden onset of heat or mild pain in a certain area of your body, or an unexpected onset of emotion or feeling. For example, you may feel heat in your stomach to indicate that someone in the group has indigestion, an ache in your foot to indicate foot pain, or a sense of depression may come upon you to indicate that someone in the group is suffering from depression. The key is to recognize that these are cues from the Holy Spirit and not your own pain or emotion.

Speak the name of the disease or affliction out loud that you hear or experience from the Holy Spirit. • Resist presumption and the urge to call out a condition that is ailing you or that you are aware that someone else in the room is suffering from unless the Holy Spirit strongly urges you to do so. • Continue to listen to the Holy Spirit for words of knowledge until you sense that He is finished.

Recorder: After your group is finished calling out all of the words of knowledge, read the entire list out loud for all the group to hear each word of knowledge again.

If you are suffering from an ailment that was called out by the words of knowledge, then raise your hand and keep it up.

Step Four: Form Small Healing Groups

Look around the room. • Assemble two or three people around each person who has raised their hand.

The person with their hand raised is the Recipient. • The people surrounding those with their hand up are the Healers. • If you have more than one person in your small group with their hand raised, then decide who will be the first to receive ministry. Leave enough time for everyone to receive healing prayer.

Recipient: Put your hand down. • Tell the Healers what infirmity that you are suffering from that was just highlighted by the Holy Spirit. • Open your heart to receive your healing as a free gift by grace through faith in Jesus Christ.

Step Five: Command Healing

Healers: (All of the instructions of this step are for the Healers.)

Don't rush! Take your time so that God's love and power can flow through you.

Look at the Recipient with compassion. • Wait in stillness and silence until you feel the love of God for them. • Believe in your heart that sickness is not God's will for them in Christ, no matter what they have done. • Remember that you are praying for God's will to be done on earth as it is in Heaven, and there is no sickness in heaven.

When you are ready, take your position of authority in Christ in your inmost being. • Believe in your heart that as a disciple of Christ, all power and authority has been given to you in Jesus' name to heal the sick.

Keep your eyes open. • While believing in your heart, command healing the way that Jesus did and believe that healing is taking place as you pray. • Use the following commands as an example:

- ♦ Be healed in Jesus' name.
- ♦ Your sins are forgiven by the blood of Jesus. Be clean in Jesus' name.
- ♦ Receive your healing in Jesus name. According to your faith, let it be done unto you.
- ♦ Deaf ears: Be opened in Jesus' name.
- ♦ Blind eyes: Be opened in Jesus' name.

As you command healing, stay alert to the promptings of the Holy Spirit. ▪ You may see pictures in your mind's eye of something that you are to do or you may feel prompted to lay your hands on the area of their body affected by infirmity. You may hear the Holy Spirit say something that you are supposed to say or ask. ▪ If what the Holy Spirit prompts you to do may cause the Recipient to be uncomfortable, tell them in advance what you believe the Holy Spirit has revealed to you and ask for the Recipient's permission to put it into practice. ▪ No matter how weird you feel, do what the Holy Spirit prompts you to do as an act of faith for the Recipient's healing.

Step Six: Examine

After commanding healing in Jesus' name, ask the Recipient to do something that they could not do before. ▪ If they have received their healing, praise God! ▪ If they received partial healing, praise God!

If the Recipient has not received their healing yet or has received partial but not full healing, then repeat Steps One, Two, Five, and Six again. ▪ Be persistent! Don't give up!

If the Recipient does not receive healing after several attempts, ask God to increase their ability to receive His love and the benefits of Christ's finished work. Bless them and let it rest for now.

Step Seven: Praise God!

Recipient: If you have received healing, praise God in the name of Jesus! Give all glory to God and not to anything or anyone else for healing you. ▪ If you have received healing for a serious diagnosed medical problem, go to the doctor to confirm your healing. ▪ Allow this healing to build your faith in God's love for you and your obedience to Christ for all that He has done for you.

Healers: If the Recipient received healing through your prayer in Jesus' name, praise God! Give all glory to God and resist the urge to take credit for yourself. Jesus is the One who healed them. ▪ Allow this healing to build your faith and obedience to Christ for more healings for more people.

Step Eight: Testify

Invite anyone in your group who is comfortable doing so to share with the group what the Lord just healed them of or any immediate results that they received or experienced.

Onward to Maturity:

Jesus healed all manner of diseases as part of His daily life as the Son of God. As children of God through faith in Christ, we can live in total health and heal others wherever we go, whenever the Holy Spirit prompts us to do so. Return to this Activity any time you or someone you know is ill or in need of healing.

The aim of this activity is be in health and to function fully
in our authority in Christ against all manner of sickness and disease.

◊ Additional Heal the Sick Activation

Anointing with Oil,[13] Laying Hands,[14] and the Prayer of Faith

Anointing with oil is symbolic of consecration to God and the power of the Holy Spirit at work. Similarly, the laying on of hands is a means of imparting righteousness, bestowing blessing or gifts, and consecrating people for God's purposes. Finally, the word for prayer used in *the prayer of faith* (see James 5:13-15) is a unique word which also denotes a special vow or consecration to God. All of this is to say that when we anoint the sick with oil, lay hands on them, and pray the prayer of faith, we demonstrate that, through faith in Jesus Christ, healing is being released by the power of the Holy Spirit because they are redeemed and set apart from all sickness so that they can carry out God's purposes. Here's how to do it:

Use anointing oil make the sign of the cross on the sick person's forehead. ▪ Lay your hand on the top of their head or on their shoulder. If the Holy Spirit prompts you to do so, lay your hands on the area of their body that is affected by sickness. ▪ Pray for them to be healed in Jesus' name. As you pray for them, believe in your heart that sickness has no place in them because they have been redeemed and set apart by the blood of Jesus to be wholly consecrated to God for His will and purposes. ▪ Praise God that by the stripes of Jesus, we were healed. Past tense. It is finished. Hallelujah!

Other Types of Healing Prayer

When praying for the sick to be healed in Jesus' name, resist prayers that beg and plead for God to do what He has already done. Keep yourself in a posture of faith that Jesus fully completed our healing by His stripes and through His death and resurrection. Resist fancy talk prayers and quoting lots of Scripture. Just command healing in the name of Jesus. Here are some additional healing command prayers that may be a helpful example for you:

- ◊ In the name of Jesus, may God's Kingdom come and God's will be done on earth as it is in heaven. There is no [name specific sickness] in heaven.
- ◊ I declare that by the stripes of Jesus, you were healed. Be healed in Jesus' name.
- ◊ Receive your healing from the top of your head to the soles of your feet in the name of Jesus.
- ◊ [Name specific infirmity], be gone in the name of Jesus. You have no place in this blood-bought child of God.
- ◊ In the power and authority of the name of Jesus, I curse all sickness in your body to its root and command it to be gone and never return.

Praise God that, by the stripes of Jesus, we were healed. Past tense. It is finished. Hallelujah!

---

[13] For a brief study on anointing with oil, see *ACTS, Chapter 2: Holy Spirit*
[14] For a brief study on the laying of hands, see *ACTS, Chapter 9: Fellowship*

ACTIVITY 11
Love Your Enemies

Jesus told His disciples to be perfect as our Heavenly Father is perfect. This includes loving our enemies the way that God loves His enemies and the way that He loved us when we were His enemies. This kind of love is only possible when the Holy Spirit and nature of Christ is working in us and through us. In this Activity, we will learn to love our enemies and bless those who curse and persecute us.

This Activity will help you to:

◊Grow in genuine love for others, even those who offend you

◊Deepen your understanding of what Christ did for you when you were God's enemy

◊Pray for those who seem to be your enemies

◊Be more like Christ and love others the way that He loves you

Step One: You Were God's Enemy

Take a moment to ponder what your life was like before you believed Jesus as your Lord and Savior or what your life could be like if He had not saved you.

Acknowledge that you were separated from God's love, in darkness, without eternal hope, suffering from vain and futile thinking, wise in your own eyes, hardened in your heart, living a life of sin, spiritually dead, and on your way to eternal damnation. • You were ungodly, lacked any spiritual strength, and were completely powerless to change your situation. • You were God's enemy.

Praise God that when you were in this condition, Jesus Christ died for you so that you could know God and be reunited with Him. • Thank God that in spite of your faults, failures, and missteps, Jesus loved you and blessed you at His own expense and without requiring any restitution or repayment from you.

Step Two: Your Enemies and Your Reactions

On a piece of paper, write down the ways that other people have treated you shamefully, cursed you, denigrated you, humiliated you, maligned your character, persecuted you, misunderstood you, or wounded you through their words and actions.

Write down the name of anyone whom you find difficult to forgive, you are holding a grudge against, evokes bitterness in you, or whom you blame for things that have impacted your life negatively.

Write down the ways that other people (their words and actions) have triggered ungodly or unloving reactions in you. These could include responses such as offense, anger, self-defense, self-justification, self-righteousness, pride, jealousy, selfish ambition, accusation, revenge, cursing them, or hoping for their failure or punishment. • For example, if you unexpectedly encountered the people that you listed above, how would you feel and what would you do? Would you be angry or annoyed? Would you withdraw or run in the opposite direction?

Step Three: Freely Receive

⚶ Invite the Holy Spirit to renew your mind and to cleanse your thoughts and motives.

Find the Love Our Enemies Actsheet. (See also: www.activatedchurch.com/actsheets) ▪ Read the *Loving Our Enemies* phrases found on the top half of the page out loud. ▪ Focus your attention on the way that God loved you when you were His enemy.

Allow several moments of stillness. ▪ Open your heart to receive God's mercy. ▪ Talk to God about any objections or resistances voiced by your intellect, flesh, religion/self-righteousness, or pride. ▪ Allow the Holy Spirit to speak to you and minister to you in these areas.

Step Four: Love Your Enemies, Freely Give

Read the *Loving Our Enemies* phrases out loud a second time. ▪ This time, focus your heart on loving your enemies the way that God loves you.

Allow several moments of stillness. ▪ Ask God to forgive you for the ungodly ways that you have reacted to the attacks and provocations of your enemies in the past. ▪ Talk to God about anything prohibiting your views towards others from being totally pure and loving.

Ask God to give you deeper revelation of His purpose for you to be like Jesus. ▪ Allow the Holy Spirit to strengthen your heart with love for your enemies.

Step Five: Pray for Your Enemies

On the Love Our Enemies Actsheet, read through the *Praying for Our Enemies* prayer supplied on the bottom half of the page. ▪ Do not pray it yet, but read it to become familiar with what the prayer entails.

Allow the Holy Spirit to highlight one of the names of people that you listed as your enemy in Step Two. ▪ As you begin to pray the *Praying for Our Enemies* prayer, fill in your enemy's name where there is a blank space.

⚶ Ask the Holy Spirit to help you to pray for your enemies.

Pray for your enemy slowly and from your heart. ▪ When it feels forced, stop, invite, and allow the Holy Spirit to minister to you and give you strength in your inmost being. ▪ If you become blocked, return to the *Loving Our Enemies* phrases to help you and repeat Steps Three and Four as needed. ▪ When your heart is genuine towards your enemy, continue praying.

Step Six: Listen for Action Steps

In the prayer above, you asked God to open your eyes, help you to love, reveal truth, help you to forgive, show you how to reconcile and make restitution, and show you how to pursue peace. ▪ Open your ears to hear what God would speak to you in response.

Allow several moments of stillness. ▪ Listen for any promptings from the Holy Spirit about what you are to do about the situation or how you may be able to bless your enemy. ▪ Allow the Holy Spirit to reveal any areas of ungodliness in you and to counsel you about how to love the way that Jesus loves. ▪ Resist the urge to come up with your own solutions or blessings. Let the Holy Spirit do the talking.

Commit yourself to following through with the instructions that God speaks to you. ▪ If you receive no action steps, then continue to pursue pure thoughts and motives towards your enemy and trust that God will show you what to do in the course of time.

Step Seven: Share

Depending on the size of your group, partner up two-by-two, gather into small groups, or do this as one large group.

As you are comfortable doing so, share what you experienced in your heart or anything new that God revealed to you by doing this Activity.

Onward to Maturity:

Perpetual and unconditional love towards our enemies is the token mark of Christlikeness and spiritual maturity. This said, we mature in our ability to love our enemies as we grow in our own comprehension of God's love for us in Christ. Return to this Activity any time you find it difficult to love, bless, forgive, or have good will toward others.

The aim of this activity is to genuinely love our enemies.

11 – *Love Your Enemies - Actsheet*
LOVING AND PRAYING FOR ENEMIES

———————————— LOVING OUR ENEMIES ————————————

While I was ungodly, a sinner, and an enemy of God, He loved me enough to die for me. Therefore, I offer love to those who are behaving in an ungodly way, sinning against God or against me, and who are behaving like my enemies or treating me wrongly.

God loves me without expecting anything from me. Therefore, I have no expectations of other people.

I received God's love as a free gift through Christ. Therefore, I do not force people to earn my love.

God does not hold a grudge against me. Therefore, I do not hold a grudge against my enemies.

Christ died to set me free from every form of oppression and bondage. Therefore, my heart's desire is for everyone, including my enemies, to be totally free in Christ.

When the things that other people say or do offend me or trigger reactions in me, I reckon that part of me dead in Christ's death so that I am free to love them the way that Christ loves me.

I believe that no one can separate me from God's love for me in Christ and that no one has the power to thwart God's plans for my life. Therefore, I am free to love others no matter what they do to me.

———————————— PRAYING FOR OUR ENEMIES ————————————

Father, in Jesus name I come to pray for _____. Thank you for bringing _____ into my life.

Thank you that you love him/her and that Jesus died for him/her. Thank you that you have a purpose for his/her life and that his/her salvation and blessing is your heart's desire.

Reveal the truth in the situation between _____ and me and let the truth set us free. Open my eyes to see _____ as you see him/her.

Father, I ask that you would show mercy to _____ and help me to be merciful them as you have been to me. Help me to forgive them from my heart as freely as you have forgiven me.

Show me how to restore and reconcile our relationship and how to be at peace with them as far as it depends on me. Reveal to me if I owe them anything and how to make restitution if necessary. Give me the strength and the courage to pursue peace at any cost.

Father, I ask for your will to be done on earth as it is in heaven where there is no division, no condemnation, no judgment, and no strife. Manifest Your love, peace, and harmony between us.

Father, in Jesus name, I ask you to bless and prosper _____'s life, family, health, and all the work of his/her hands. Make Yourself known to _____ in deeper ways and reveal Your unconditional love to him/her.

Father, help me to love _____ the way that you love me.

ACTIVITY 12
In God's Presence

Jesus maintained a continual abiding in the presence of God and told His disciples to do likewise. In this Activity, we will practice soaking in the presence of God in order to take steps toward full-time abiding.

This Activity will help you to:

◊ Let go and let God be in control

◊ Become more comfortable with stillness

◊ Hear what the Lord may be whispering to you

◊ Receive from the Lord whatever He desires to give to you

◊ Be refreshed with renewed faith, hope, and love

Introduction: Soaking[15]

Jesus said that only one thing was needed for our sustenance as we follow Him. When Mary sat at His feet, positioned to hear, receive, and partake of everything that Jesus may convey to her, He said that she chose the better portion and that it would not be taken away from her.

Soaking in the presence of God is essentially doing the same thing that Mary did. When we soak in God's presence, we stop focusing on other things, let go of control, and allow God to speak to us anything that He may want to share with us. Through this, we receive more than we would have asked for and what we receive remains with us forever.

Step One: Prepare

Music: If you have live worship available, ask the worship leaders to play softly and keep lyrics to a minimum. ▪ If you do not have live worship, Christian soaking music is readily available for purchase. Otherwise, almost any Christian worship music will do. ▪ Test in advance to be sure that your music player is able to fill your space with music so that everyone can hear. ▪ Try to silence distracting noises as much as possible.

Alert the members of your group in advance to wear comfortable clothing. ▪ Arrange your space to be as cozy as possible.

Designate one person to be the time-keeper who will alert everyone when the soaking time is complete.

Ask everyone to turn off all of their electronic devices or anything that may disturb or distract the soaking time.

---

[15] For more on soaking or a prayer trance, see *ACTS, Chapter 12: Devotion*

Note: Soaking is an opportunity for everyone to have one-on-one time with Jesus even though you are in the room together. Therefore:

- ♦ Refrain from speaking or whispering to others during the soaking time, even if you believe that you have a revelation from the Lord for them.
- ♦ If you see someone crying, leave them alone and let them cry. The Lord is most likely ministering to their heart.
- ♦ If you see someone that has fallen asleep, let them sleep until the soaking time is completed. God does some of His best work when we rest deeply in Him.
- ♦ If you struggle with extended stillness, ask the Holy Spirit to help you or meditate on the verse, "Be still and know that I am God." (Psalm 46:10)

Step Two: Soak and Receive (20 minutes)

Have everyone find their own comfortable place to sit, stand, or lay down within your meeting room. • They may want to bring their Bible with them or bring a pen and paper in order to write down anything that the Lord may reveal to them.

♦ Invite the Holy Spirit to come and minister to you however the Lord sees fit. • Open your hearts to receive all that the Lord has for you in this time.

Begin playing the music. • Open your heart to receive from the Lord. • You can close your eyes or keep them open. • Listen and receive all that He reveals, heals, speaks, and imparts to you. Keep the eyes of your heart open to seeing any visions that He wants to show you. Listen for anything that He directs you to do.

Allow for 20 minutes to pass while you soak and receive from the Lord. • Have the time-keeper alert the group that time is completed or turn the music off. • Slowly return to your regular group seating.

Step Three: Write Insights

On a piece of paper, take a moment to write down one thing that you believe God revealed to you during your time in His presence. If you are unsure of any one thing, make a note of how you feel after being in His presence for an extended time.

Step Four: Share

Depending on the size of your group, partner up two-by-two, gather into small groups, or do this as one large group.

As you are comfortable doing so, share something new that God revealed to you by doing this Activity and how it will change the way you pursue a relationship with God from now on.

Onward to Maturity:

Return to this Activity any time you need to be revived or refreshed in the Lord's presence. Practice soaking for more extended periods of time and then practice being in God's presence even when you are not physically being still. As we grow in Christlikeness, our abiding in the Lord's presence becomes deeper and more unbroken no matter what we are doing.

The aim of this activity is to abide in God's presence at all times.

♦Additional In God's Presence Activation[16]

Prayer

To pray in God's presence, invite the Holy Spirit to guide your prayer time and then be still and wait for Him to direct you. ▪ Listen for whatever the Lord directs you to pray about or bring specific issues or situations to Him. Ask Him for wisdom and then be still and wait for Him to speak. ▪ When He speaks, pray into what is revealed by asking Him for more clarity and allowing Him to speak. ▪ Continue in this type of dialogue until He stops speaking about that issue. ▪ Bring your next issue to Him for prayer or remain in a posture of listening in case He directs your attention to another topic.

Fasting

Fasting is the act of abstaining from food in order to voluntarily submit yourself to bodily weakness so that Christ is magnified within you. ▪ As you engage in a full or partial fast from food, focus your attention on the presence of the Lord and receiving all that He has to share with you. ▪ When your craving for food intensifies, seek to deepen your abiding connection with the Lord instead of eating.

Study of the Word of God

To study the Scriptures in God's presence, invite the Holy Spirit to direct your time of study and follow wherever He leads you. ▪ Ask the Holy Spirit to reveal Christ to you in every passage of Scripture. ▪ Ask for revelation of all that Christ accomplished for you and died to give you. ▪ Keep a notebook nearby to take notes.

[16] For more on prayer, fasting, and study of God's Word, see *ACTS, Chapter 12: Devotion*

ACTIVITY 13
Tending Soils

As we follow Jesus, we will face tests and trials which are the evil one's attempts to thwart the plan of God for our lives. When we discern the enemy's schemes, we are strengthened in our ability to resist evil and to stand firm in our faith in Christ so that we receive all that He has for us. In this Activity, we are going to examine various and general tactics of the enemy against God's words to us.

This Activity will help you to:

- Maintain a heart of faith in God's words to us
- Discern the schemes of the enemy
- Persevere and stand firm through various trials
- Produce the fruit of righteousness with honesty and goodness
- Receive everything that Christ died to give us

Introduction: Not Missing It[17]

In the Book of Acts, Stephen gave a speech outlining various times throughout the course of Israel's history when they had missed what God was doing. Of course, this speech culminated by pointing out that they had failed to recognize Jesus as their Messiah and had crucified Him instead. In short, they did not understand God's ways, they feared the rejection of others, they could not stand firm when things became difficult, and they were too immersed in the world and its ways to recognize their own King.

To be fair, there are times when all of us miss God or fail to recognize what He is doing in our lives. In fact, Jesus taught a parable to His disciples which reveals the various ways that the enemy attempts to prevent us from carrying out God's purposes and receiving all that Christ died to give us. It is good for us to be aware of these enemy schemes so that we can stand firm in our faith and not miss what God is doing.

This Activity is based on the Parable of the Sower which can be found in Matthew 13:1-23; Mark 4:1-24; and Luke 8:4-18. As Jesus explained, the seed is the word of God or the word of the Kingdom of God and the soils represent the various conditions of our hearts.

Step One: Snatched Seed

The first soil in Jesus' parable is the soil along the path. This soil represents hearts that hear the word of the Kingdom and do not understand it. The evil one comes quickly to snatch away the seed before it has

---

[17] For in-depth teachings on soils and missing God, see *ACTS, Chapter 2: Holy Spirit* and *Chapter 13:Types & Shadows*

even entered the ground. • Practically speaking, when the enemy schemes to snatch the seed of God's word out of the soil of our hearts, we will think things such as:

- ◊ Was that God or was that me? (i.e. *"Did God really say…"*)
- ◊ That doesn't make any sense to me. It doesn't seem to be safe, wise, intelligent, or practical.
- ◊ I don't think that is the way that God would do it.
- ◊ I can't do that.
- ◊ I do not believe that it will work out.
- ◊ Maybe I am making that up. Maybe that is my pride, fear, or secret desire speaking but not God.

Ask the Holy Spirit to bring to remembrance times in the past that you may have unknowingly allowed the enemy to snatch a seed out of your life. • For example:

- ◊ Did you believe Jesus as your Lord and Savior the first time you heard the Gospel?
- ◊ Has God ever asked you to do something that did not make sense to you and, therefore, you decided not to do it?
- ◊ Was there ever a word from the Lord that you found too hard to believe so you ignored or dismissed it?

Allow for several moments of stillness and silence as the Holy Spirit reveals your personal history with snatched seeds. • Take a moment to apologize to God for not understanding what He had been doing in those times in the past. • Receive His forgiveness through the blood of Jesus.

Moving into the present, ask the Holy Spirit to bring to remembrance the words from the Lord that are significant to your life right now. • Consider: Are you struggling to believe because you do not understand? • Could it be that the enemy is trying to snatch the word away from you?

Take a few moments to submit yourself afresh to God. • Ask for God to speak to give you wisdom and revelation as you grow in your knowledge of Him. • Let go of your need to understand or have it all figured out. • Resist the evil one's attempts to snatch the word of God away from you.

Step Two: Tribulation and Persecution

The second soil in Jesus' parable is the soil on rocky ground. This soil represents hearts that hear the word of the Kingdom and receive it with joy but have no root system. When tribulation or persecution comes, they quickly fall away rather than standing firm. • Practically speaking, when the enemy schemes to cause seed failure through persecution and tribulation, we will experience things such as:

- ◊ People do not agree with what God has told you to do. (i.e. *"Did God really say…"*)
- ◊ Everything in your life starts falling apart, particularly in the area of God's word.
- ◊ People distance themselves from you or reject you for following God's word, even friends and family.
- ◊ Your life begins to look like the exact opposite of what God said to you.
- ◊ Self-persecution thoughts like: "Who do I think I am?" and "What will people think of me?"
- ◊ Persecution from others for believing God and His word, even friends and family.

 ♦ People telling you that you have lost your mind or that God's word will fail you, even friends and family.

Ask the Holy Spirit to bring to remembrance times in the past that you may have unknowingly allowed for seed failure due to harassment and hardship. • For example:

 ♦ Someone you respect or love told you that you couldn't or shouldn't do what God told you to do, so you decided not to do it.

 ♦ The circumstances in your life became so overwhelming that you gave up or stopped believing that you had heard God.

 ♦ Following God's word would have caused too much trouble in your relationships, so you decided not to pursue it for the sake of peace.

 ♦ You were afraid of what people would think of you, so you decided it was best not to obey God.

 ♦ You were bullied or teased by others for doing what God told you to do, so you stopped in order to make their bullying stop.

Allow for several moments of stillness and silence as the Holy Spirit reveals your personal history with failed seeds due to fear of man and adversity. • Take a moment to apologize to God for not being able to stand firm through those trials in the past. • Receive His forgiveness through the blood of Jesus.

Moving into the present, ask the Holy Spirit to bring to remembrance the words from the Lord that are significant to your life right now. • Consider: Are you struggling to believe because people misunderstand you? Are you struggling to believe because things in your life do not appear to be going your way? • Could it be that the enemy is trying to cause you to fall away from believing?

Take a few moments to submit yourself afresh to God. • Ask for God to cause the roots of your faith to grow down deeply in the love of Christ. • Let go of the need for other people's approval. • Shift your focus off of your circumstances and onto Jesus who endured through the cross to receive God's promised reward. • Resist the evil one's attempts to cause your faith to fail through persecution and tribulation.

Step Three: This World and Money

The third soil in Jesus' parable is the soil among thorns. This soil represents hearts that hear the word of the Kingdom but become distracted by money and the cares of this world. This soil is unable to grow to maturity or bear any fruit. • Practically speaking, when the word of God is being choked in our lives, we will think things such as:

 ♦ I do not believe that God wants to me to pay that price for Him. (i.e. *"Did God really say…"*)

 ♦ That costs too much, I can't afford to do that, or it's too risky.

 ♦ I have to work for a living, I have to eat, or I have responsibilities.

 ♦ Doing this would not be good for my reputation.

 ♦ I'll do it after I get my degree, raise my kids, have enough money, or have enough time.

 ♦ I do not want to give up the power, influence, money, and possessions that I have worked so hard to attain.

- ⟡ God accepts me the way that I am. I am comfortable and I do not want to change.
- ⟡ I want God to bless my life without me having to change the way that I do things.

Ask the Holy Spirit to bring to remembrance times in the past that you may have unknowingly stunted your spiritual growth due to money or the ways of this world. • For example:

- ⟡ You were afraid to trust God to provide financially for what He asked you to do, so you did not do it.
- ⟡ You compromised what God told you to do to in order to suit your comfort.
- ⟡ You delayed your obedience to God's instructions due to practical concerns.
- ⟡ You were unwilling to give something because it would have caused you financial strain.
- ⟡ You did not want to sacrifice money or status because you thought you had earned it.
- ⟡ You were afraid to trust God to guard your reputation.
- ⟡ You did not want to change the lifestyle that you had grown accustomed to.

Allow for several moments of stillness and silence as the Holy Spirit reveals your personal history with choked seeds. • Take a moment to apologize to God for not being willing to sacrifice or being able to trust Him through those trials in the past. • Receive His forgiveness through the blood of Jesus.

Moving into the present, ask the Holy Spirit to bring to remembrance the words from the Lord that are significant to your life right now. • Consider: Do you feel stunted in your growth with the Lord? Is there anything that He has asked you to sacrifice or to trust Him with but you have not been willing? Is there anything that you would do right away for the Lord if money were not a concern? • Could it be that the enemy is trying to choke the word of God from bearing fruit?

Take a few moments to submit yourself afresh to God. • Ask God to help you to be willing to pay the cost of being a disciple of Jesus. • Let go of your need for financial security. Let go of the desire for a life which blends in with your culture. • Resist the evil one's attempts to cause your faith to fail through persecution and tribulation.

Step Four: Good Soil, Letting the Seed Die

The last soil in Jesus' parable is the good soil. This soil represents hearts that hear the word of the Kingdom, receive it, understand it, and perseveres through various trials to bear mature fruit. This soil bears 30, 60, and 100-fold fruit of righteousness for Christ and the Kingdom of God. In another passage of Scripture, Jesus explains that a seed must fall to the ground and die before it is able to bear fruit, but that if it dies it is able to bear much fruit. • Practically speaking, when we hear the Word of God and persevere in faith while also allowing the seed to fall to the ground and die, we:

- ⟡ Maintain a steadfastness of faith in our hearts in spite of all outward signs to the contrary.
- ⟡ Let go of our own thoughts and ideas about how God is going to bring His word to pass.
- ⟡ Get out of God's way so that His will is done and our fruitfulness is multiplied.

Ask the Holy Spirit to bring to remembrance a time in your walk with the Lord that you knew that you knew that you had heard Him and you did not allow anything or anyone to convince you otherwise until you received what He had promised you. • Remember how you let go of how you thought it would be or how God delivered in a different way than you were expecting. • Praise God for His faithfulness in being true to His word.

Moving into the present, ask the Holy Spirit to bring to remembrance the words from the Lord that are significant to your life right now. • Reaffirm your faith in Him and what He has spoken to you. • Imagine yourself allowing the seed to fall to the ground and die so that it can become what God intends. • Offer yourself entirely to God as a living sacrifice and invite Him to have His way in your life. • Ask God to give you deeper knowledge of His will and to strengthen you with the patience and endurance that you will need in order to see it all the way through to fulfillment.

Step Five: Share and Pray

Gather into small groups or partner up with one other person. • Share with one another the one soil that you have the most personal history with. • If you are comfortable doing so, share how this Activity will change the way that you discern and resist the schemes of the enemy from now on.

Pray for one another to submit to God and to resist the devil and his various schemes. • Ask for God to increase your discernment of good and evil. • Ask God to increase your revelation of our inheritance in Christ and all that He died to give us freely by grace. • Ask God to help you to stay heavenly minded and focused on eternal rather than temporal rewards.

Onward to Maturity:

Discernment of good and evil is one of the marks of spiritual maturity. Return to this Activity any time you find yourself doubting the word of the Lord to you or feel stunted in your progress for any reason. Keep in mind the heroes of the faith listed in the Book of Hebrews (a list which includes Jesus) who endured through many and various trials because they believed the word of God to the fullest. If we believe and endure as they did, we will receive all that God has promised us.

The aim of this activity is to discern the schemes of the enemy
so that we can resist the devil and receive all that Christ died to give us.

ACTIVITY 14
Teach, Preach, Testify

Jesus proclaimed the Gospel of the Kingdom of God and sends us out as His witnesses to go and do likewise. In this Activity, we will practice teaching, preaching, and testifying as witnesses of what Jesus has done for us. This way, we will always be ready to give a reason for our faith in Christ.

This Activity will help you to:

    ♭ Use the Scriptures to explain the good news of Jesus Christ

    ♭ Persuade unbelievers of God's love for them in Christ

    ♭ Testify about what Jesus has done in your life

    ♭ Discern the best way to witness for Christ in various situations

Introduction: My Witnesses[18]

In a court of Law, a witness testifies for or against someone or something based on what they know about that person or situation. In short, they affirm through all means available what they have seen, heard, or experienced. As Christ's witnesses to the world, we are equipped with power from heaven to teach from the Scriptures, preach the Gospel of the Kingdom, and testify about what Jesus has done in our lives. The Holy Spirit gives us wisdom to share Christ effectively in various ways depending on who we are speaking to, no matter who we encounter.

Note: This Activity purposefully gives equal exposure to teaching, preaching, and testifying. If you desire for your group to concentrate on any one of these areas, then focus exclusively on that portion of this Activity and allow for more time, reflection, and sharing with one another. Practice teaching, preaching, and testifying to one another by designating some people to play the role of the audience being witnessed to.

Important Note: Please be certain not to leave out Step Five so that you go out into the world to witness for Christ to those who need it the most.[19]

Step One: Teach

Ask the Holy Spirit to help you to select one of the following audiences:

    ♭ A Jewish person that does not believe that Jesus is their Messiah

    ♭ Someone who knows the Scriptures but has wandered away from the faith

    ♭ A disciple of Christ who is struggling with unbelief

Ask the Holy Spirit to help you to select one of these Scripture passages:

---

[18] For an in-depth teaching on being Christ's Witnesses, see *ACTS, Chapter 14: My Witnesses*

[19] For basic witnessing techniques, see *Additional Teach, Preach, Testify Activation* at the end of this chapter

Isaiah 53:1-12	Job 14:7-17	Psalm 118:14-24	Galatians 4:15-29
Psalm 22:1-31	Psalm 110	Leviticus 16	Romans 4:12-21
John 3:13-18	Matthew 13:24-30	Exodus 15:1-18	Colossians 1:15-23
1 Corinthians 1:18-31	1 Timothy 1:12-17	Romans 8:1-17	2 Timothy 2:8-13

Read the Scripture passage that the Holy Spirit has highlighted for you. • Ask the Holy Spirit to give you revelation within the Scripture passage of how Jesus made a way for believers to know God and what Jesus accomplished for us through His death and resurrection.

Consider for a moment the audience that the Holy Spirit highlighted for you. • Ask the Holy Spirit to show you how to communicate with them the way that Jesus would.

With the help of the Holy Spirit, create a teaching using the Scripture passage and audience that the Holy Spirit highlighted for you. • Write down your full teaching or bullet points, or simply meditate on what you would say.

Allow 5-7 minutes or an appropriate amount of time for your group. • After the time is up, pause for a moment.

Ask the Holy Spirit to bring to mind someone who fits the description of the audience that you have chosen. • If possible, reach out to the person this week or ask God to make a way for you to share this teaching with them.

Step Two: Preach

Ask the Holy Spirit to help you to select one of the following audiences:

- ◊ A person who is an atheist
- ◊ An agnostic person who believes that all forms of spirituality are the same
- ◊ A Jewish person that does not believe that Jesus is their Messiah
- ◊ A disciple of Christ who is struggling with unbelief

Consider for a moment the audience that the Holy Spirit highlighted for you. • Ask the Holy Spirit to show you how to communicate with them the way that Jesus would.

Ask the Holy Spirit to show you how to preach or tell the Good News of God's love for us in Jesus Christ to the audience that the Holy Spirit highlighted for you. • Do not use any specific Scriptures to communicate your beliefs and do not reference your personal experience. Try to use something that they believe as a starting point. • Write down the full text of what you would say, write down bullet points, or simply meditate on how you would preach the Good News.

Allow 5-7 minutes or an appropriate amount of time for your group. • After the time is up, pause for a moment.

Ask the Holy Spirit to bring to mind someone who fits the description of the audience that you have chosen. • If possible, reach out to the person this week or ask God to make a way for you to share this teaching with them.

Step Three: Testify

God's mercy and grace are often best revealed through us when we tell the story of how we used to be the worst of sinners. (1 Timothy 1:12-17)

Ponder in your heart the ways that you were the worst of sinners before you knew Jesus as your Lord and Savior. • If you struggle with identifying yourself this way, ask the Holy Spirit to help you to see the way that you used to be. Were you proud, self-pitying, wild, manipulative, mean, angry, helpless, hopeless, or evil?

Ponder in your heart the ways that God's love has changed you. • Include the ways that Jesus has been faithful to you through the course of time as you have walked with Him.

Imagine yourself sharing your testimony of Jesus with a perfect stranger. • Write down your testimony, bullet points, or simply meditate on what you would say. • Ask the Holy Spirit to help you highlight the most important parts.

Allow 5-7 minutes or an appropriate amount of time for your group. • After the time is up, pause for a moment.

Step Four: Share

Depending on the size of your group, partner up two-by-two, gather into small groups, or do this as one large group. • In your groups, consider and discuss your answers to the following questions:

- ♦ Was teaching, preaching, or testifying the easiest for you? Why?
- ♦ Was teaching, preaching, or testifying the hardest for you? Why?
- ♦ In what ways do you find it challenging to share Christ with unbelievers?
- ♦ What is one thing God revealed to you through doing this Activity that will change the way you witness for Christ?

Pray for one another to be strengthened as witnesses for Jesus Christ and the Kingdom of God. • Ask God to give you boldness to proclaim the Gospel and to stretch out His hand to do miracles, signs, and wonders to glorify the name of Jesus.

Step Five: Listen and Go!

Ask the Holy Spirit to give you specific words of knowledge about people that God wants you to share the Gospel with right away (or as soon as you see them.) These could be:

- ♦ Family members or close friends (by name)
- ♦ Acquaintances or people that you work with (by name)
- ♦ Description of a person so that you know them when you see them (i.e. lady in a red dress or handy man)
- ♦ Descriptions of a struggle that a person is having so that you know when you encounter someone who is facing this trial (i.e. recently divorced or death in the family)
- ♦ Places for you to go to share the Gospel (i.e. the corner of 1st & Main Street or Varanasi, India)

Allow a moment of stillness and silence to let the Holy Spirit speak. ▪ Listen for who God brings to mind or what God describes to you or reveals in prophetic pictures and make a note of it. ▪ Commit to contacting these people this week or go out and find them where God has told you to look. (See Additional Activation for some basics of witnessing in this way.)

Ask God to open doors of opportunity this week for you to teach, preach, and testify about Jesus. Ask Him to give you boldness to proclaim the Good News about Jesus. ▪ In all of your encounters, ask the Holy Spirit to show you how to best share the Gospel with the person that you are witnessing to. Be prepared to teach, preach, or testify as the Holy Spirit guides you.

Onward to Maturity: Witness 24/7

Stay alert at all times to the promptings of the Holy Spirit about sharing the Good News of Jesus Christ with anyone that the Lord may cause you to encounter. It could be the person next to you on the bus, your waitress at a restaurant, or a good friend who has never been willing to listen before. If you sense that the Holy Spirit is directing you to share Christ with someone, trust that God will give you the right words to say. Then, speak from your heart. Be kind, keep it simple, and leave the results in God's hands.

The aim of this activity is to know and proclaim the Gospel of Jesus Christ.

◊Additional Teach, Preach, Testify Activation

Salvation Available to All

Ask the Lord to create opportunities for you to share the Gospel of Jesus Christ everywhere you go. The Gospel is the most inclusive message and is available to everyone from every nation, rich or poor, young or old, and from any religious background. Everyone who confesses with their mouth that Jesus is Lord and believes in their heart that God raised Him from the dead will be saved. (see Romans 10:9)

This said, believing Jesus Christ as Lord and Savior is a life-changing decision and lifetime commitment which should not be taken lightly or forced upon anyone. Jesus did not command us to go and make converts but to go and make disciples who genuinely believe and follow Him. Therefore, when someone is ready to believe Jesus as their Lord and Savior, confirm that they believe that Jesus is Lord and that God raised Him from the dead. Also, make sure that they know that this is a serious decision that will impact the rest of their life. Then, lead them in a prayer of salvation so that they are certain that, starting today, they have placed their faith in Jesus Christ and have been welcomed into the family of God. Ask them to repeat after you and pray something like this:

Salvation Prayer

Heavenly Father, I come to you in Jesus' name.
Forgive my past and help me to be a new person.
I believe that Jesus is Lord and that God raised Him from the dead.
Fill me with your Holy Spirit and guide me into your will for my life.
Starting today, I believe that I am a child of God because Jesus Christ is my Lord and Savior.
Amen.

After you have led someone in the salvation prayer, welcome them into the Kingdom and the family of God. Encourage them to do these things as soon as possible:

- ◊ Get water baptized as an outward sign of the beginning of their new life in Christ.
- ◊ Tell someone that they prayed a prayer of faith in Jesus.
- ◊ Get a Bible and begin reading it.
- ◊ Find a church and get involved with other people who believe in Jesus.

Offer to help them in any way that you can. Don't be forceful; be helpful. Love them the way that Jesus loves you.

Starting the Conversation

Depending upon how the Lord positions you to witness to various people, it can sometimes be uncomfortable to start a conversation about Jesus. Here are some general ways of breaking through the awkwardness.

◊ Love:

In all of your witnessing, always remember that the best way to reveal Christ to someone is by simply loving them unconditionally. Be kind, be honest, be sincere, and be genuine. ▪ Evangelism is not a sales pitch. Have no agenda except to love them. ▪ When the time is right, or when they ask, tell them about Jesus and His love. Tell them that because you love them, you want them to know Jesus too. ▪ If they are not ready to listen, keep on loving them until they are.

◊ Prayer:

If it becomes clear in the course of ordinary conversation that the person that you are speaking with is struggling with something in their life right now, ask them if you can pray for them in Jesus' name. ▪ If they agree to prayer, then pray for them freely.

When you are finished praying, ask them if they know Jesus or if they believe that Jesus is Lord. ▪ As they respond, listen to the Holy Spirit for the best way to share the Gospel with them. ▪ If they are ready to reaffirm their faith in Christ or to place their faith in Jesus for the first time, lead them in the salvation prayer.

If it becomes clear that they are not ready to take the next steps towards faith in Christ, thank them for allowing you to pray with them for the situation in their life and ask them to let you know what God does. Then, move on and trust that you have planted a seed that God will cause to grow.

◊ Word of Knowledge:

If the Holy Spirit gives you a word of knowledge about someone or something that they are going through, find a way to deliver the message from God to them. ▪ Start by saying something like, "I'm sorry if this seems weird, but I'm sensing that [describe what God revealed to you]. Would it be alright for me to pray for you in Jesus' name?" If you know that they are more open to the things of God, then you can say something like "God loves you so much that He has given me a message for you. [Describe what God revealed to you]."

When you are finished sharing the word of knowledge with them, ask them if they know Jesus or if they believe that Jesus is Lord. ▪ As they respond, listen to the Holy Spirit for the best way to share the Gospel with them. ▪ If they are ready to reaffirm their faith in Christ or to place their faith in Jesus for the first time, then lead them in the salvation prayer.

If it becomes clear that they are not ready to take the next steps towards faith in Christ, reaffirm how much God loves them to send you to deliver a message to them. Then, move on and trust that you have planted a seed that God will cause to grow.

◊ Supernatural Encounter:

If the Holy Spirit has led you to witness to someone through a supernatural encounter (i.e. healing, deliverance, dream interpretation, in-depth prophetic word, etc.), be sure to invite them to know Jesus as their Lord and King. ▪ In this case, because the Lord has done something miraculous for them, make sure that they know that this is a full life commitment to following Jesus before they agree to pray. ▪ If they agree that they are ready to give their life to Jesus, pray the salvation prayer with them.

If it becomes clear that they are not ready to take the next steps towards faith in Christ, affirm their decision to count the cost of following Jesus and ask them if you can pray for them to have a deeper experience of the love of God. Then, pray something like, "Father, in Jesus' name, I ask you to give [their name] an encounter with your love so that they will come to know you." Then, move on and trust that you have planted a seed that God will cause to grow.

ACTIVITY 15
The Aim

The aim of the Christian life is to be like Jesus so that we fulfill God's eternal purpose. In order to do this, we need to discern good and evil so that we are free to obey God with a pure faith and right motives. In this Activity, we will identify and resist the false beliefs, erroneous practices, and misdirected ambitions so that we can stay on the narrow path of Christ and God's will for us.

This Activity will help you to:

- Grow in discernment of good and evil
- Renounce false beliefs, practices, and aims
- Test the spirit behind various teachings
- Examine motives for godliness or error
- Reset and maintain your focus on Christ alone

Introduction: Becoming Like Christ[20]

This Activity includes an examination of our lives for certain sins and erroneous beliefs. This is not for the purpose of creating paranoia or excessive focus on the schemes of the devil but rather to equip us to discern good from evil so that we can receive Christ's mercy and pursue His likeness. While it is true that our sin has been fully paid for by Christ's sacrifice, there are certain beliefs, practices, and teachings that Jesus warned us to beware of and the apostles of the early church determined to be detrimental to Christ's disciples. We must be alert to such things in order to abide in truth, keep our hearts softened to God's voice, believe the true Gospel, and maintain a clear conscience. Sin and error are dangerous, not because Christ rejects us for them but because they cause us to become susceptible to rejecting Him and forfeiting our eternal inheritance. As we allow the Holy Spirit to renew our minds towards faith in God in every area of our lives, He transforms us and causes us to become like Christ.

This Activity utilizes several Actsheets. See www.activatedchurch.com/actsheets for printable pdf files.

Step One: The Aim is Christ

Find the Aim Actsheet #1, *the Aim is Christ*. ▪ Designate one person to be the Reader or decide to rotate around the group with each person reading one Scripture passage.

Reader(s): Read the Scriptures out loud at a slow pace.

Listen carefully with your heart to the words and ways of God.

---

[20] For an in-depth study on false beliefs, wrong practices, and incorrect aims, see *ACTS, Chapter 15: Yeast*

Step Two: False Beliefs

Jesus warned His followers to beware of the yeasts of the Pharisees, Sadducees, and Herod or religion, unbelief, and worldliness, respectively. Just like yeast spreads and permeates through a whole batch of dough, false beliefs have a tendency to spread into every facet of our lives until we no longer worship Jesus in spirit and in truth. If we persist in wrong beliefs, we become susceptible to rejecting Jesus just like the hypocrites and the world did.

◊ Invite the Holy Spirit to come and to examine your heart.

Find the Aim Actsheet #2, *False Beliefs*. ▪ Note: These are the categories of false beliefs that Jesus warned His followers to beware of and keep out of our lives.

Glance over the chart of false beliefs. ▪ Ask the Holy Spirit to highlight or draw you into one category. Within that category, allow the Holy Spirit to bring one false belief to your attention.

With that belief in mind, ponder and do your best to answer the questions below. ▪ As you ponder your answers, keep your spiritual ears open for the Holy Spirit's assistance. ▪ If you are struggling to answer the question, then ask God to reveal it to you by asking for wisdom. ▪ As needed, use the Scriptures provided underneath the chart or allow the Holy Spirit to bring to remembrance relevant Scriptures that may not be listed.

> ◊ In what way is this not like Jesus?
> ◊ In what ways could this belief be dangerous or damaging to me or others?
> ◊ What would I be like if this belief became dominant in my life?
> ◊ In what way does this belief distort the message of the Gospel?
> ◊ If it was revealed that I believe this, how could it impact my credibility as a witness for Christ?

Allow 5 minutes or an appropriate amount of time for your group. ▪ After the time is up, pause for a moment.

Ask and allow the Holy Spirit to reveal truth and to renew your mind from old ways of thinking, particularly this false belief. ▪ Return to the Scriptures on the *Aim is Christ* Actsheet as a guide or any other Scriptures that the Holy Spirit brings to mind.

Ask God to show you how to trust Him and the sufficiency of Christ's sacrifice. ▪ Pray something like this:

> *"Father, thank you for sending your Son, Jesus, to pay for my false beliefs by His blood. In Jesus' name, I ask that you cleanse my mind from [state your wrong belief] and give me revelation of everything that was accomplished for me by the death and resurrection of Jesus so that my trust and faith are in Christ alone."*

Step Three: Wrong Practices

Wrong practices in our lives wage war against our souls. Over time, repetitive violation of God's ways causes our hearts to become hardened and our ears to become deaf to the whisper of the Holy Spirit. If we persist in indulging in error in our lives, we depart from the narrow way of Christ and become susceptible to rejecting Him entirely.

Find the Aim Actsheet #3, *Wrong Practices and Incorrect Aims* and focus on the *Wrong Practices* section found on the top half of the page. • Note: These are the categories of wrong practices determined by the first apostles to be particularly damaging to believers and the Church.

Glance over the chart of wrong practices. • Ask the Holy Spirit to highlight or draw you into one category. Within that category, allow the Holy Spirit to bring one false belief to your attention.

With that practice in mind, ponder and do your best to answer the questions below. • As you ponder your answers, keep your spiritual ears open for the Holy Spirit's assistance. • If you are struggling to answer the question, then ask God to reveal it to you by asking for wisdom. • As needed, use the Scriptures provided underneath the chart or allow the Holy Spirit to bring to remembrance relevant Scriptures that may not be listed.

- ◊ In what way is this not like Jesus?
- ◊ In what ways could this practice be dangerous or damaging to me or others?
- ◊ What would I be like if this practice became dominant in my life?
- ◊ In what way does this practice distort the message of the Gospel?
- ◊ If it was revealed that I do this, how would it impact my credibility as a witness for Christ?

Allow 5 minutes or an appropriate amount of time for your group. • After the time is up, pause for a moment.

Ask and allow the Holy Spirit to reveal truth and to renew your mind from old ways of thinking, particularly this wrong practice. • Return to the Scriptures on the *Aim is Christ* Actsheet as a guide or any other Scriptures that the Holy Spirit brings to mind.

Ask God to give you strength to renounce this wrong practice forever. • Pray something like this:

> *"Father, thank you for sending your Son, Jesus, to pay for my wrong practices by His blood. In Jesus' name, I ask that you strengthen me with your power in my mind, will, and emotions to overcome [state your wrong practice] forever."*

Step Four: Incorrect Aims

Incorrect aims in our hearts have the ability to lead us into deception and to steer us off of the course of God's will for our lives. Continually making choices that are based on reaching or attaining anything other than Jesus and being like Him causes us to lose sight of God's eternal purposes. If we persist in pursuing wrong objectives, we make ourselves or our target to be a god in place of Christ. This is what the apostle Paul called *a different gospel*. • Note: Not all incorrect aims are bad things. Some of the things that we target are good things or may be bi-products of following Christ and only become errant when we regard them and strive after them as our ultimate objective or mark of success.

On the Aim Actsheet #3, focus on the *Incorrect Aims* section found on the bottom half of the page. • Note: There are so many erroneous objectives that it is not possible to supply them all on this chart. Use this statement as a test: The aim is _____ so that I learn to trust in _____. If your target leads you to trust in anything other than God or to measure your success by anything other than being like Jesus, then your aim is incorrect.

Glance over the *Incorrect Aims* chart. • Allow the Holy Spirit to bring one incorrect aim to your attention.

With that aim in mind, ponder and do your best to answer the questions below. • As you ponder your answers, keep your spiritual ears open for the Holy Spirit's assistance. • If you are struggling to answer the question, ask God to reveal it to you by asking for wisdom. • As needed, use the Scriptures provided underneath the chart or allow the Holy Spirit to bring to remembrance relevant Scriptures that may not be listed.

- ◊ In what way was this not Jesus' objective?
- ◊ In what ways could this aim be dangerous or damaging to me or to others?
- ◊ What would I be like if this aim became dominant in my life?
- ◊ In what way does this aim distort the message of the Gospel?
- ◊ If it was revealed that this is my aim, how would it impact my credibility as a witness for Christ?

Allow 5 minutes or an appropriate amount of time for your group. • After the time is up, pause for a moment.

Ask and allow the Holy Spirit to reveal truth and to renew your mind from old ways of thinking, particularly this incorrect aim. • Return to the Scriptures on the *Aim is Christ* Actsheet as a guide or any other Scriptures that the Holy Spirit brings to mind.

Ask God to show you how to stay focused on His will and purpose for your life. • Pray something like this:

> *"Father, thank you for sending your Son, Jesus, to die for my incorrect aims by His blood. In Jesus' name, I ask that you would reveal your purpose for my life to me and help me to stay focused on Jesus so that I never aim for [state your incorrect aim] again."*

Step Five: Share

Depending on the size of your group, partner up two-by-two, gather into small groups, or do this as one large group.

As you are comfortable doing so, share something new that God revealed to you by doing this Activity and how it will change the way you follow Christ from now on.

Ongoing: Consider Carefully What You Listen to

Exercise and develop your discernment of good and evil by listening carefully to your own thoughts and to what other people say, particularly those seeking to influence your life and beliefs. • As you listen, ask the Holy Spirit to help you to answer the following questions:

- ♦ Who or what is the god of this thought?
- ♦ Who or what is being emphasized as the most important thing?
- ♦ Who or what am I being asked to place my faith and trust in or depend upon?
- ♦ If trust in God and the sufficiency of Christ's sacrifice is not being promoted, then what is?

Use Steps One, Two, and Three of this Activity to test the substance of the thought or belief being presented. As you do this, you will increase your ability to keep yourself free from false beliefs, wrong practices, and incorrect aims so that you can pursue God's will and Christ's likeness.

Onward to Maturity:

As you walk with God and grow in Christlikeness, return to this Activity as you encounter or struggle with false beliefs, wrong practices, or incorrect aims. Anytime you seem to be off the path of God's will for your life, use this Activity to help you to renew your mind and to redirect your steps. The Holy Spirit will help you to stay on track by bringing to remembrance the words of Christ and by leading you in all truth so that you receive everything that Christ died to give you.

The aim of this activity is to discern good and evil so that we are free to fulfill God's eternal purposes.

15 – *The Aim - Actsheet #1*
THE AIM IS CHRIST

Selection of Scriptures

So do not worry, saying, 'What shall we eat?' or 'What shall we drink?' or 'What shall we wear?' For the pagans run after all these things, and your heavenly Father knows that you need them. But seek first his kingdom and his righteousness, and all these things will be given to you as well. {Mathew 6:31-33}

Jesus gave them this answer: "Very truly I tell you, the Son can do nothing by himself; he can do only what he sees his Father doing, because whatever the Father does the Son also does. {John 5:19}

"If anyone comes to me and does not hate father and mother, wife and children, brothers and sisters-- yes, even their own life--such a person cannot be my disciple. And whoever does not carry their cross and follow me cannot be my disciple. {Luke 14:26-27}

Jesus called them together and said, "You know that the rulers of the Gentiles lord it over them, and their high officials exercise authority over them. Not so with you. Instead, whoever wants to become great among you must be your servant, and whoever wants to be first must be your slave--just as the Son of Man did not come to be served, but to serve, and to give his life as a ransom for many." {Mathew 20:25-28}

Jesus went throughout Galilee, teaching in their synagogues, proclaiming the good news of the kingdom, and healing every disease and sickness among the people. {Mathew 4:23}

Jesus answered, "The work of God is this: to believe in the one he has sent." {John 6:29}

Once you were alienated from God and were enemies in your minds because of your evil behavior. But now he has reconciled you by Christ's physical body through death to present you holy in his sight, without blemish and free from accusation-- if you continue in your faith, established and firm, and do not move from the hope held out in the gospel. This is the gospel that you heard and that has been proclaimed to every creature under heaven, and of which I, Paul, have become a servant. {Colossians 1:21-23}

And that is what some of you were. But you were washed, you were sanctified, you were justified in the name of the Lord Jesus Christ and by the Spirit of our God. "I have the right to do anything," you say--but not everything is beneficial. "I have the right to do anything"--but I will not be mastered by anything. {1Corinthians 6:11-12}

For we do not have a high priest who is unable to empathize with our weaknesses, but we have one who has been tempted in every way, just as we are--yet he did not sin. {Hebrews 4:15}

"My food," said Jesus, "is to do the will of him who sent me and to finish his work. {John 4:34}

The aim of the Christian life is to be like Jesus in order to fulfill God's eternal purpose.

15 – The Aim – Actsheet #2
FALSE BELIEFS

──────── **FALSE BELIEFS** ────────

Category	Beliefs
Religion *Yeast of the Pharisees*	Believing that God's blessings are earned and deserved
	Criticizing imperfections or practices of others and looking down on others
	Following rules or standards in order to be good or approved by God
	Saying one thing but doing another
	Practicing traditions which negate the commands of God or are not rooted in His Word
	Twisting God's Word to suit personal desires and ambitions
Unbelief *Yeast of the Sadducees*	Doubting or not believing in God's ability or power to do something
	Doubting or not believing in God's good nature or willingness to bless
	Controlling outcomes rather than trusting God or trusting in "doing the right thing"
	Not believing in the infallibility of the Scriptures
	Lack of knowledge or ignorance of God's Word
	Not believing that God works miracles today or in the resurrection from the dead
	Aligning with governing/political authorities or regarding them as the ultimate power
Worldliness *Yeast of Herod*	Indulging in unrestrained sin and/or abusing God's grace
	Aiming for or measuring results based on the world's standards of success
	Basing personal security and self-worth in financial sufficiency and possessions
	Believing that money and possessions are the sign of success or failure
	Making a name for yourself or pursuing personal fame, power, influence, or dominance
	Utilizing prowess, might, or manipulation to rule or lord over people
	Believing in or adhering to philosophies which are not rooted in Christ and His sacrifice (i.e. knowledge of good and evil, common sense, human cunning, craftiness, etc.)
	Believing in or adhering to forms of spirituality which are not rooted in Christ (i.e. horoscopes, karma, secret knowledge, visualization, witchcraft, sorcery, etc.)

Selection of Scriptures

1 Tim 6:10	Matt 7:21-23	Romans 12:2	Mark 9:23
John 3:18	1 John 2:4	Colossians 3:2	John 15:18-19
1 John 2:15-17	Revelation 21:8	Titus 2:12	James 1:27
2 Tim 3:5	Matthew 26:52	James 4:4	Matt 6:5-24
Titus 1:16	Ephesians 2:8-9	Matt 23:13-31	Matt 7:1-5
Matt 20:25-28	James 2:10	Matt 10:8	2 Thess 2:10-12

False beliefs spread into every area of our life until we no longer worship Jesus in spirit and truth.

15 – *The Aim- Actsheet #3*
WRONG PRACTICES AND INCORRECT AIMS

--------------------- WRONG PRACTICES ---------------------

Category	Practices
Idol Worship	Giving higher priority to things, people, or tasks than to God
	Coveting or focusing affections or ambitions on things or people other than Christ
	Believing in other gods, religions, or spirituality and/or adhering to their practices
	Relying on anything but Christ for salvation, deliverance, healing, or sustenance
	Eating food that has been offered to other gods or to idols
Sexual Immorality	All forms of sex outside of marriage between one man and one woman
	Lust, pornography, and wrong ideas about sex and its purpose
	Using sex to manipulate or substituting sex for love
Disregard for Life	Cruelty towards people or living creatures (i.e. deliberately inflicting pain, neglect)
	Deliberate oppression, humiliation, or indifference
	Consuming or misusing blood

Selection of Scriptures

Acts 15:29	1 Peter 2:11	1 John 5:21	James 4:2-4
Romans 8:13	1 John 3:4	Matt 26:52	Ephesians 5:3-7
Matt 5:28	Romans 12:19	1 John 3:15	Matt 15:19-20
Hebrews 13:4	Revelation 21:8	Colossians 3:5	1 Tim 1:9-11
Gal 5:19-21	1 Cor 6:9-10, 18	1 Cor 10:14	1 Thess 4:3-8

Wrong practices harden our hearts and deafen our ears to the whisper of the Holy Spirit.

--------------------- SAMPLE OF INCORRECT AIMS ---------------------

Being Good	Knowledge	Money	Status	Praise of Men
Serving	Me, Myself, and I	Influence	Relationships	Activism/Causes
Business Results	Leadership	Good Works	Gifts/Abilities	Brokenness
Morality	Entertainment	Theology	What I Want	Family
Cultural Standards	Power/Miracles	Career	Community	Education

The aim is _____ so that I learn to trust in _____ .

Selection of Scriptures

1 John 2:15-17	2 Tim 3:2-5	Titus 2:12	Hebrews 13:5
Matthew 6:24	Romans 12:2	Matt 10:8	Matt 10:38-39
Luke 14:26	Colossians 3:2	Matt 20:25-28	2 Tim 2:22
2 Cor 10:3-5	Galatians 1:8-9	2 Cor 11:4	1 Cor 1:26-31

Incorrect aims lead us into deception until we believe a different gospel.

ACTIVITY 16
40 Day Reset

Jesus said that He could do nothing by Himself without His Father and that we as His disciples can do nothing without Him. He submitted Himself entirely as a servant of God and a slave of righteousness and did nothing which was not in alignment with God's will. In this Activity, we will open our lives up to a Holy Spirit reset so that we can walk more fully in the obedience of faith.[21]

This Activity will help you to:

◊ Align yourself with God's will and purposes for your life

◊ Deepen your alertness and submission to the Holy Spirit

◊ Replace your own ways of doing things with God's ways

◊ Extract activities out of your life that God did not initiate

◊ Walk more fully in the will of God for your life

Step One: Prepare in Advance

Find the 40 Day Reset Actsheet at the end of this chapter. (See also: www.activatedchurch.com/actsheets for an easy to print pdf file.) ▪ Follow the instructions on the top of the page so that there are enough prayers cut out and available for each person in the group. ▪ The Actsheets are set up to align with one another to create two-sided prayer sheets. The prayer is the front side and the 40 Day Reset commitment is the back side. ▪ If two-sided copies are not possible, the front side alone is sufficient. ▪ If you do not have copying or printing capacity at all, follow the instructions given in Step Four of this Activity.

Step Two: Commit to Reset

◊ Invite the Holy Spirit to come and to lead you in paths of righteousness.

Read through the 40 Day Reset commitment below.

Over the course of the next 40 days, I commit to:

◊ Listen to God's promptings and do what He says

◊ Allow God to prune out of my life everything that He did not initiate

◊ Release back to God anything that He did initiate but that I have taken control of in my flesh

◊ Let go of anything that I am not certain is God's will so that God can confirm it to me

◊ Stop presuming that I know what God would do and stop finishing God's sentences

◊ Place my faith entirely in the power of God and not in the wisdom of men

◊ Try to do only what God desires for me to do

---

[21] For an in-depth study on walking in obedience, see *ACTS, Chapter 16: God's Guidance*

Only do this if you believe genuinely in your heart that you desire to do only God's will for your life and are ready to commit to following through. ▪ Read through the 40 Day Reset commitment again but, this time, use your own words to say it to God in the form of a prayer.

Allow a moment of stillness and silence. ▪ Listen for anything that the Holy Spirit reveals to you that God desires for you to start doing or anything that God desires for you to stop doing. ▪ Write down what God reveals to you and commit to following through, no matter what happens.[22]

Step Three: Mark Your Calendar

Count off 40 days on your calendar, using today as Day 1. ▪ Mark Day 1 and Day 40 on your calendar.

Decide if you desire to have weekly or daily reminders so that you do not forget about your commitment to reset between now and Day 40. ▪ Mark your calendar with however many reminders you decide are appropriate for you.

Step Four: Select a Reset Prayer

Have each person in the group select one of the Actsheet prayers at random out of the basket or bag which was prepared in advance.

Note: If you do not have the ability to make copies, have everyone partner up with one other person and allow your partner to choose for you one of the three prayers listed on the Actsheet. ▪ On a piece of paper, write the prayer that your partner has selected for you.

Pray this prayer for yourself every day for the next 40 days. ▪ Keep your Reset Prayer piece of paper with you or keep it in a place where you will see it daily.

Step Five: Review

On Day 40, ask the Holy Spirit to help you to look back and see what adjustments God has made to your life.

Take note of things or people that have been added to or removed from your life. ▪ Take note of anything that surprises you about what was revealed during your 40 Day Reset.

Praise God for leading you into better alignment with His will and purpose for your life. ▪ Ask Him to help you to walk in alignment with His will and purposes for the rest of your life.

Optional: Group Reset

Repeat Steps Two through Five for your group as a whole.

Listen together to the Holy Spirit for how God desires to realign your group with His purposes. ▪ Maintain an open dialogue and include everyone in the discussion regarding God's will for your group.

Select one Reset Prayer for your group and have everyone pray it for your group for 40 days.

After reviewing what God revealed in the 40 days, commit to following through with all that God

---

[22] See Additional Reset Activation at the end of this chapter for a helpful meditation

revealed to you.

Onward to Maturity:

Jesus said that not everyone who calls Him Lord will enter the Kingdom of Heaven but only those who do the will of the Father. Jesus always did what was pleasing to God and empowers us through the Holy Spirit to do likewise. Return to this Activity any time you need to reset your course on God's will or realign your priorities with God's purposes.

The aim of this activity is to do only the will of the Father so that we enter into the Kingdom of God.

16 – 40 Day Reset - Actsheet
RESET PRAYERS - FRONT

Divide the number of people in your group by 3. • Make that many copies of this page. • For example, if you have 18 people in your group, 18 ÷ 3 = 6, so you would make 6 copies of this sheet. These Actsheets can be accessed on the web at: www.activatedchurch.com/actsheets

Cut along dotted lines and discard the excess. • Fold each prayer in half and place them in a basket or bag. • Allow each person to select one prayer at random out of the basket or bag. • This will be their Reset Prayer for the next 40 days.

- -

I pray that out of his glorious riches he may strengthen you with power through his Spirit in your inner being, so that Christ may dwell in your hearts through faith. And I pray that you, being rooted and established in love, may have power, together with all the Lord's holy people, to grasp how wide and long and high and deep is the love of Christ, and to know this love that surpasses knowledge--that you may be filled to the measure of all the fullness of God. Now to him who is able to do immeasurably more than all we ask or imagine, according to his power that is at work within us, to him be glory in the church and in Christ Jesus throughout all generations, for ever and ever! Amen. {Ephesians 3:14-21}

- -

We continually ask God to fill you with the knowledge of his will through all the wisdom and understanding that the Spirit gives, so that you may live a life worthy of the Lord and please him in every way: bearing fruit in every good work, growing in the knowledge of God, being strengthened with all power according to his glorious might so that you may have great endurance and patience, and giving joyful thanks to the Father, who has qualified you to share in the inheritance of his holy people in the kingdom of light. For he has rescued us from the dominion of darkness and brought us into the kingdom of the Son he loves, in whom we have redemption, the forgiveness of sins. {Colossians 1:9-14}

- -

I keep asking that the God of our Lord Jesus Christ, the glorious Father, may give you the Spirit of wisdom and revelation, so that you may know him better. I pray that the eyes of your heart may be enlightened in order that you may know the hope to which he has called you, the riches of his glorious inheritance in his holy people, and his incomparably great power for us who believe. That power is the same as the mighty strength he exerted when he raised Christ from the dead and seated him at his right hand in the heavenly realms, far above all rule and authority, power and dominion, and every name that is invoked, not only in the present age but also in the one to come. And God placed all things under his feet and appointed him to be head over everything for the church, which is his body, the fullness of him who fills everything in every way. {Ephesians 1:17-23}

- -

16 – *40 Day Reset* - *Actsheet*
RESET COMMITMENT - BACK

---

40 Day Reset – I commit to:

- Listen to God's promptings and do what He says
- Allow God to prune out of my life everything that He did not initiate
- Release back to God anything that He did initiate but that I have taken control of in my flesh
- Let go of anything that I am not certain is God's will so that God can confirm it to me
- Stop presuming that I know what God would do and stop finishing God's sentences
- Place my faith entirely in the power of God and not in the wisdom of men
- Try to do only what God desires for me to do

---

40 Day Reset – I commit to:

- Listen to God's promptings and do what He says
- Allow God to prune out of my life everything that He did not initiate
- Release back to God anything that He did initiate but that I have taken control of in my flesh
- Let go of anything that I am not certain is God's will so that God can confirm it to me
- Stop presuming that I know what God would do and stop finishing God's sentences
- Place my faith entirely in the power of God and not in the wisdom of men
- Try to do only what God desires for me to do

---

40 Day Reset – I commit to:

- Listen to God's promptings and do what He says
- Allow God to prune out of my life everything that He did not initiate
- Release back to God anything that He did initiate but that I have taken control of in my flesh
- Let go of anything that I am not certain is God's will so that God can confirm it to me
- Stop presuming that I know what God would do and stop finishing God's sentences
- Place my faith entirely in the power of God and not in the wisdom of men
- Try to do only what God desires for me to do

⬧Additional Reset Activation

The Red Sea Situation (see Exodus 14)

Asking God to reset our lives from the way that we are already living to the way that He wants our lives to be can sometimes feel overwhelming and impossible. Use this meditation to build your faith in God's ways over your own practical ways of thinking about the situation, trial, or circumstance in your life right now that seems impossibly difficult to you.

⬧ Ask the Holy Spirit to help you to see with the eyes of your heart.

THE RED SEA SITUATION	YOUR CURRENT SITUATION
Imagine yourself standing by the banks of the Red Sea with approximately two million Israelites. You are hemmed into an impossible situation with the waters of the Red Sea on one side of you and the Egyptian army closing in on the other side of you.	Think about your current situation. Acknowledge to God how impossible it looks from your viewpoint.
Think with your logical mind about what solutions you might come up with for the Red Sea Situation. Would you build boats? Go to battle? Pray for God to strike your enemies with lightning?	Apply this to your current situation. Ponder for a moment the solutions that you have come up with in your natural way of thinking.
God instructed the Israelites to be still and to trust the He was fighting for them. Imagine yourself being still and trusting God in the face of such danger.	Apply this kind of faith to your current situation. Let go of your own man-made solutions. Be still and listen for God's instructions.
Next, God instructed Moses to lift up his staff in faith and believe that God was going to do the unthinkable and even the impossible.	Lift up your hands in faith while believing in your heart that God is able and willing to help you in your situation in His own ways.
Finally, God parted the waters of the Red Sea and walked all the Israelites through on dry ground but their enemies were completely drowned.	Reaffirm your faith in God's ability to do the impossible. Envision yourself walking through your current situation untouched by your enemies.
After God walked the Israelites through the Red Sea Situation, they sang a song of praise to God for all that He had done for them. (see Exodus 15)	When God walks you through your current situation, praise Him for all that He has done for you. Better yet, start praising Him now for what He has already done.

MY PRAYER

May we all offer ourselves in absolute surrender to following God's guidance through the indwelling Holy Spirit.

> *{Rom 12:1-2} Therefore, I urge you, brothers and sisters, in view of God's mercy, to offer your bodies as a living sacrifice, holy and pleasing to God--this is your true and proper worship. Do not conform to the pattern of this world, but be transformed by the renewing of your mind. Then you will be able to test and approve what God's will is--his good, pleasing and perfect will.*

May we all press onwards in our devotion to Jesus so that we become mature in Christ, accomplish all that He has prepared for us, and receive everything that He died to give us.

> *{Phl 3:12-16} Not that I have already obtained all this, or have already arrived at my goal, but I press on to take hold of that for which Christ Jesus took hold of me. Brothers and sisters, I do not consider myself yet to have taken hold of it. But one thing I do: Forgetting what is behind and straining toward what is ahead, I press on toward the goal to win the prize for which God has called me heavenward in Christ Jesus. All of us, then, who are mature should take such a view of things. And if on some point you think differently, that too God will make clear to you. Only let us live up to what we have already attained.*

May we all grow in our revelation knowledge of our inheritance in Christ Jesus, the power of God, and His purpose for us as His Church.

> *{Eph 1:17-23} I keep asking that the God of our Lord Jesus Christ, the glorious Father, may give you the Spirit of wisdom and revelation, so that you may know him better. I pray that the eyes of your heart may be enlightened in order that you may know the hope to which he has called you, the riches of his glorious inheritance in his holy people, and his incomparably great power for us who believe. That power is the same as the mighty strength he exerted when he raised Christ from the dead and seated him at his right hand in the heavenly realms, far above all rule and authority, power and dominion, and every name that is invoked, not only in the present age but also in the one to come. And God placed all things under his feet and appointed him to be head over everything for the church, which is his body, the fullness of him who fills everything in every way.*

May we all as the Church, including all of Christ's disciples from every nation in the earth, be united as ONE so that we reveal the love of Jesus to the world.

> *{Jhn 17:20-23} [Jesus praying] "My prayer is not for them alone. I pray also for those who will believe in me through their message, that all of them may be one, Father, just as you are in me and I am in you. May they also be in us so that the world may believe that you have sent me. I have given them the glory that you gave me, that they may be one as we are one-- I in them and you in*

me--so that they may be brought to complete unity. Then the world will know that you sent me and have loved them even as you have loved me.

May we all be ACTIVATED to become the Church of Acts. Hallelujah!!

ABOUT THE AUTHOR

Wendy Bowen was the ultimate Type A, workaholic, overachiever, and control-freak until she had a dramatic encounter with the Lord Jesus Christ. Since then, the Lord called Wendy to give away all of her possessions and live by faith, prayer, and obedience to His voice. She lives for the purpose of proclaiming the Gospel and building up the Church by teaching the Word of God, helping believers experience Jesus through the Holy Spirit, and equipping disciples in their Kingdom purpose. The Lord blesses her ministry with His manifest presence and with miracles, signs, and wonders.

www.activatedchurch.com

www.ingramcontent.com/pod-product-compliance
Lightning Source LLC
LaVergne TN
LVHW081328060426
835513LV00012B/1226